IMMERSION
Bible Studies
ROMANS

Lynn H. Cohick

Abingdon Press

Nashville

ROMANS
IMMERSION BIBLE STUDIES
by Lynn H. Cohick

Copyright © 2011 by Abingdon Press

Library of Congress Cataloging-in-Publication Data
Cohick, Lynn H.
   Romans / Lynn H. Cohick.
     p. cm. —(Immersion Bible studies)
   ISBN 978-1-4267-0986-9 (curriculum—printed/text plus-cover, adhesive - perfect binding : alk. paper)
   1. Bible. N.T. Romans—Textbooks. I. Title.
   BS2586.P68 2010
   227'.107—dc22

2010051256

Editor: Mark Price
Leader Guide Writer: John P. "Jack" Gilbert

11 12 13 14 15 16 17 18 19 20—10 9 8 7 6 5 4 3 2

Manufactured in the United States of America

IMMERSION
Bible Studies

ROMANS

Praise for Immersion

"Immersion Bible Studies is a powerful tool in helping readers to hear God speak through Scripture and to experience a deeper faith as a result."
     Adam Hamilton, author of *24 Hours That Changed the World*

"This unique Bible study makes Scripture come alive for students. Through the study, students are invited to move beyond the head into the heart of faith."
     Bishop Joseph W. Walker, author of *Love and Intimacy*

"If you're looking for a deeper knowledge and understanding of God's Word, you must dive into Immersion Bible Studies! Whether in a group setting or as an individual, you will experience God and his unconditional love for each of us in a whole new way."
     Pete Wilson, founding and senior pastor of Cross Point Church

"This beautiful series helps readers become fluent in the words and thoughts of God, for purposes of illumination, strength building, and developing a closer walk with the One who loves us so."
     Laurie Beth Jones, author of *Jesus, CEO* and *The Path*

"I highly commend to you Immersion Bible Studies, which tells us what the Bible teaches and how to apply it personally."
     John Ed Mathison, author of *Treasures of the Transformed Life*

"The Immersion Bible Studies series is no less than a game changer. It ignites the purpose and power of Scripture by showing us how to do more than just know God or love God; it gives us the tools to love like God as well."
     Shane Stanford, author of *You Can't Do Everything . . . So Do Something*

Contents

Review Team

IMMERSION BIBLE STUDIES

A fresh new look at the Bible, from beginning to end,
and what it means in your life.

Welcome to IMMERSION!

We've asked some of the leading Bible scholars, teachers, and pastors to help us with a new kind of Bible study. IMMERSION remains true to Scripture but always asks, "Where are you in your life? What do you struggle with? What makes you rejoice?" Then it helps you read the Scriptures to discover their deep, abiding truths. IMMERSION is about God and God's Word, and it is also about you—not just your thoughts, but your feelings and your faith.

In each study you will prayerfully read the Scripture and reflect on it. Then you will engage it in three ways:

Claim Your Story
> Through stories and questions, think about your life, with its struggles and joys.

Enter the Bible Story
> Explore Scripture and consider what God is saying to you.

Live the Story
> Reflect on what you have discovered, and put it into practice in your life.

IMMERSION makes use of an exciting new translation of Scripture, the Common English Bible (CEB). The CEB and IMMERSION BIBLE STUDIES will offer adults:

- the emotional expectation to find the love of God
- the rational expectation to find the knowledge of God
- reliable, genuine, and credible power to transform lives
- clarity of language

Whether you are using the Common English Bible or another translation, IMMERSION BIBLE STUDIES will offer a refreshing plunge into God's Word, your life, and your life with God.

1.

God Credits Us As Righteous— in Spite of Ourselves

Romans 1–4

Claim Your Story

"Love means never having to say you're sorry." This line from the novel *Love Story* was made famous by the movie of the same name. But nothing could be farther from the gospel truth. This proverb does, however, express the human hope that others will accept us as we are. What are we really like? What must we admit is our "human condition"?

The opening chapters of Romans leave the reader with no illusions: each human has in one form or another turned his or her back on the Creator God. If that was the only point of these chapters, this would be a sad story indeed. But the resounding note is one of great joy, for our sinful predicament does not have the final word. If I could rephrase that movie sentiment, I might say, "Love means no longer having our sins held against us." And I might add, "Love means never being outside of God's forgiving grace." What if sometimes you don't feel forgiven? Or what if you don't feel you need to be forgiven? Paul answers both these questions: God's salvation plan includes everyone, and God does not play favorites.

Enter the Bible Story

Paul opens his letter to the Romans describing himself as "a slave of Christ Jesus." With this label he claims absolute allegiance to God the Father and God's Son Jesus Christ, and he acknowledges his freedom from this present (evil) age and from sin's power. Paul will encourage the Romans to embrace their status as slaves of righteousness (6:18) and live out their freedom, for they are no longer slaves to sin (6:20). Paul also explains that he was called to be an apostle to the Gentiles, proclaiming the good news promised in Scripture and completed in the work of Jesus Christ. God defeated death and, thus, sin's power in the resurrection of God's Son. Jesus' human lineage from David, and David's from Abraham, links Jesus with the story of the Creation, Fall, and Redemption. Paul focuses on Abraham and his faith in Chapter 4; here he notes that Jesus is the fulfillment of God's promises to David (see 2 Samuel 7:12-16).

Paul's thanksgiving sections often preview the main points of his letter. Notice in Romans 1:8-14 that Paul stresses his desire to meet the Roman church and to preach the good news of salvation to those in Rome. Paul especially focuses on reaping a harvest among Gentiles. No one knows who began the church in Rome, but most likely Jews from Rome traveled to Jerusalem for Pentecost and there heard Peter preach and became followers of Jesus (Acts 2:1-41). When they returned to Rome, they established a fellowship within their synagogues. Gentiles who feared God were welcome. Then, under Emperor Claudius, many Jews were expelled from Rome, including those who worshiped Christ. The church was a Gentile community for five years, until the new Emperor Nero rescinded the order. Jewish Christians returned, but the re-integration was rocky. Today we too have a tendency to prefer fellowship with people quite similar to ourselves and to resist change brought by new members in our group. Paul encourages us to reach beyond our prejudices and embrace others.

The Heart of the Gospel

In Romans 1:16, Paul lays out the heart of the gospel. Several points must be noted. First, what we translate as *gospel* is in Greek literally *good news*. We celebrate God's redemption in Christ every time we say the word. Second, Paul declares that God's good news has full supremacy—it breaks the power of death and brings salvation. In Paul's day the competing argument was that Caesar would bring peace and harmony. Today we often hear that persons can get in touch with their inner selves and find serenity. Yet, in truth, only God's work in Christ can bring the peace that touches the deepest longings of the human heart. Third, Paul indicates that God's salvation is to the Jew first and then to the Greek. Why is this statement important? It connects Paul's message of salvation tightly to the prior revelations of God to Israel and to the Jews of the Second Temple period. The gospel message is the fulfillment of God's promises. Not only is each of us individually redeemed through Christ's work on the cross, but we are also united as members of God's family. Twenty-first-century individualism can deaden our ears to the wonderful news that God has made God's followers into a family. Paul reminds us that we are part of a very long line of faithful followers of God. We read of God's faithfulness to past believers, and we have assurance that all the struggles of our day are not too big for God. Moreover, these struggles can be faced together, as God's church.

About the Scripture

Romans and Martin Luther

One of the giant figures of the Protestant Reformation, Martin Luther, was immensely influenced by the Book of Romans. In fact, Luther considered his break-through in understanding a crucial sentence in Romans 1:17—*"The righteous person will live by faith"*—to be like a conversion experience. For it assured him at last that faith alone, not works, was the sole requirement for being made right before God. Due in large part to Luther's encounter with Romans, the Latin term *sola fide* ("faith alone") became the touchstone of Luther's life and faith, as well as a key tenet of Reformation theology.

Romans 1:17-18 are parallel in thought, and several key terms are either repeated ("revealed") or contrasted, such as "righteous" and "unrighteous," and "God's righteousness" and "God's wrath." In these verses, Paul expands the list of pairs from thinking only of Jew and Gentile, to including the righteous and the unrighteous—this second pair does not map exactly onto the first pair. Instead, from both Jews and

Gentiles we find righteous and unrighteous. Today this claim—that believers come from any nationality and ethnic group—is an accepted reality. But Paul was preaching this good news to the first generation of people to hear of God's redemption for all peoples in Christ. In Paul's day, any Jew would (rightly) consider a Gentile as an idolater and, thus, as unrighteous. And the Jews would (again, rightly) consider themselves as righteous in that they were not idolaters but followed the one true God. Paul accepts this as the truth, but not the whole truth. Jews in Christ cannot place the law of Moses (Torah) on an equal footing with the work of Christ. Now in Christ, Gentile idolaters can be made right with God without having to embrace the Mosaic law.

What Went Wrong

Paul sets out in the remaining verses of Chapter 1 to describe how and why things went so terribly wrong with God's good creation. He makes two charges against human beings: (1) they did not honor God and (2) they did not thank God. Instead they made idols, which, as the Bible clearly shows, led to all manner of wrongdoing (sin). Consequently, God turned humanity over to its sinning not because God stopped loving humanity, but because God is forbearing (9:22-24) and fair. We continue to erect idols of stone and wood today—we worship human achievements or out of fear we cling to our possessions. We dishonor God with our focus on what we (wrongly) think we can do for ourselves and we fail to thank God for God's care.

In Paul's day, Jewish believers reading this section of Romans would have recognized aspects of Israel's history (recall the golden calf incident, Exodus 32:7-8). Certain Gentiles likewise shared Paul's disdain for the evils described in Chapter 1: disobeying parents, murdering, ruthlessness, and deceitfulness. Paul's imagined conversation partner, "every single one of you who judge" (2:1), could be a Jew or Gentile, but one who prides himself or herself on seeking the truth and acting honorably. God is impartial, Paul declares (2:11), and will judge each person at the end of time based on whether each person sought truth (honored and thanked God) or promoted self to the center and pursued wickedness. The second half of Chapter 2 is difficult to understand if one supposes that Paul is speaking here about the universal sinfulness of humanity. The passage begins to make a bit more sense if we remember that Paul is dealing not only with the categories of Jews and Gentiles, but with a third entity— the Gentile believer, who is no longer a pagan but is also not a Jew. Paul finds that Gentile believers, though not born Jews and, thus, not naturally part of God's covenant people, behave in line with the law because they are living in Christ. So we, too, if we have God at our center and not our selves, walk in God's way, displaying from our hearts and hands humility, generosity, and loving-kindness.

The Law Is Not Enough

Speaking directly about Jews in 2:17, Paul criticizes his Jewish compatriots for boasting in their Jewish ethnic status. It is not enough that God called Israel and gave them the law. The Jews must also *do* what the law says—refrain from stealing and adultery, for example. Nor would Jews disagree with Paul at this point, for first-century Jewish writings argue extensively about how best to do God's law. But Paul takes the argument in a specific direction; his charge is Gentile rejection of God based on the Jews' transgression of the law (2:24). Paul concludes that circumcision, that special rite that distinguishes Jew from Gentile, is not finally the determining factor in God's judgment. Consider how that plays out in our own day: do we not set up special requirements in addition to faith in Christ, such as church membership perhaps, or a specific form of baptism, or even speaking in tongues? Are we not guilty of confusing our own personal values for spiritual markers of acceptance in God's family?

Paul knows of a new category of person, the uncircumcised (Gentile) who follows the law (2:26). Such a person will be justified, that is, saved on the Last Day. This category breaks new ground—it fulfills old promises such as Jeremiah 31:33 that God will put God's law in their minds and write it on their hearts. Foreshadowing later discussion in Chapters 7 and 8, Paul contrasts Spirit and letter, circumcision of the heart and of the flesh to drive home the point that Gentile believers fulfill the law and thus will be judged righteous. How is this possible? Paul's answer comes in the next chapter.

The question opening Chapter 3 is whether the Jew has any advantage. Paul has two competing truths that he must balance: (1) God chose Israel and gave it the law, and (2) God shows no partiality. By entrusting the law to Israel, God gave the Jewish people the opportunity to know God through God's self-revelation. They also had greater responsibility to live out that law. Their faithlessness in regard to that accountability does not nullify God's faithfulness or just requirements. The key is that both Jews and Gentiles are under the power of sin (3:9). We all share the same fate, death, because we are all sinners. Paul cites a composite quotation that draws from several Psalms and the prophet Isaiah to prove his point. Paul's statement in 3:20 that through the law sin is fully recognized would receive a hearty "Amen" from his fellow Jews. It is Paul's claim that works of the law will not justify that would have created the controversy. The phrase "works of the law" (NIV) has been understood in two basic ways. It could mean all the requirements of the law or be limited to those requirements that serve to distinguish Jew and Gentile, such as circumcision, food laws, and sabbath practices. In either case, Paul is suggesting that while the law is good (see also 7:12), it has not been understood properly and must now be understood in light of Christ's work, to which Paul now turns.

The Gift of Salvation in Christ Is Sufficient

Some of the most theologically complex verses are contained in Romans 3:21-31. And as such, at a certain level of detail they are also the most contested. But the main points are clear: Christ through his death on the cross and his resurrection from the dead defeated sin. God through Christ has accomplished salvation and offers it to all humans. Not everyone today would hold, with Paul, that humanity's main problem is sin. Some suggest that the lack of self-actualization is the primary problem. Others see in Paul's pronouncement an exclusivity that strikes them as unloving, and so they believe that life with God (or in "heaven") after death should be the reward of every "good" person. These positions, however, fail to fully comprehend the depth of sin in each person's heart, for no one fully honors God or thanks God as they should. Also these views do not appreciate the wonderful news stressed by Paul that God offers the free gift of salvation to everyone. All humans have full access to Christ's work through faith. This "faith" is not a "work" of its own, nor is it an emotional connection made with God, nor anything else generated by human effort. It is rather the joyful response to God's gracious gift (3:24). God demonstrates God's righteousness by offering this free (yet costly) gift of salvation apart from following the commands of the law. Said another way, our faith stance is the proper way to uphold the law, because God is the God of all.

Abraham: The Father of All Who Believe

Anticipating counter arguments, Paul pulls out his trump card in Chapter 4. Abraham, the father of the Jews, is also the father of all who believe. Romans 4 has been interpreted in two general ways. One position holds that Abraham is a model of our Christian faith, the prototype of *how* an individual is made right with God (saved). Rather than relying on one's own moral good deeds (actions), a person relies on faith, and then God considers or declares that person to be righteous. Another position suggests that Abraham's story shows *why* Gentiles can be full members of God's family. In first-century Judaism, most Jews thought of themselves as children of Abraham (see Matthew 3:9; 22:32; Luke 13:16; 19:9; John 8:39), and they pointed to their circumcision as proof. This status made them members of God's covenant people. However, Paul argues that Abraham's circumcision was a sign or a seal of something that happened earlier, namely that Abraham believed God's promise to make him the father of many nations. Abraham trusted that God would do what God promised; do you have that same trust? We can believe God when God says that forgiveness is better than bitterness, for God gives us grace to forgive. We can trust God's word that God will provide for us, so we need not live in worry and anxiety. Jesus' words in the Sermon on the Mount (Matthew 5:1–7:29) provide a picture of what it looks like to live out Abraham's faith that God fulfills God's promises.

Across the Testaments

Abraham

Abraham is introduced in Genesis 11:26, and in the next chapter is called and blessed by God. God promises Abraham offspring as numerous as the dust of the earth and the land of Canaan to which God is leading him (13:14-17). This promise is repeated in 15:1-5, where Abraham's offspring are to be as numerous as the stars in the heavens. In 15:6, God declares Abraham righteous because of his faith. Thirteen years later, when Abraham is ninety-nine years old, God establishes circumcision as the sign of God's covenant promise (17:1-14).

The contrast Paul makes is not between faith and works of self-righteousness. Later in the chapter Paul specifies circumcision as the deed in question and makes clear that this deed does not make one righteous or a member of God's faithful community. The contrast is between faith and unbelief. Abraham believed that God could make him a father, though humanly both he and his wife Sarah were past the age of childbearing. Abraham believed God's promise, and thus was credited as righteous. The order of events is crucial for Paul. If God had first ordered Abraham circumcised and then gave him the promise, Paul's argument falls flat; for God would have credited righteousness to Abraham based on works—circumcision. Of course, circumcision came after the faithful response of Abraham; and God's declaration of "not guilty" came not through circumcision, but through Abraham's belief in God's promises. Paul declares that the ground is level at the foot of the cross. To those of us today who have trouble believing fully that the church community is our home because we are conscious of our waywardness, Paul's words offer comfort and confidence that it is our faith, our reception of God's great gift that opens the way to membership in God's family. And to those who have lived long in the church, Paul's words remind us anew that the doors remain open to all who call upon the name of the Lord in faith.

Live the Story

In some families it is very clear who the favorite child is, the one who can do no wrong, who gets the special presents and privileges. Paul addresses that mentality in these chapters in Romans. He makes clear that God shows no partiality. That can cut both ways. From a positive angle, this truth reassures each of us that God's power alone, that great force that raised Christ from the dead, has acted on our behalf. Our sin is fully accounted for in Christ and we are considered righteous by God. We must hear this refrain loud and clear—All sins are paid for by Christ's work on the cross, and God has declared to each believer the verdict: NOT GUILTY! But there is another side to the statement that God shows no partiality. The church must offer the gospel to all people as potential brothers and sisters in Christ.

Consider your church community: where do you see attempts to put up pseudo-markers of spiritual status that act as barriers to the gospel? Does your congregation welcome (shun) the single mother or the mentally challenged young man or the unruly child or the socially marginalized or the ones whose views rub up against the majority?

At the same time, justification by faith according to Paul does not mean that believers are now free to do as they please. Dietrich Bonhoeffer in his book *The Cost of Discipleship* calls that "cheap grace," describing believers grown lazy in their obedience to God because of the false notion that salvation by grace requires neither repentance nor discipleship. Nothing could be farther from Paul's mind. How would you describe your own faith at this very moment? What does the idea that you have been made righteous by God evoke in you? How would you evaluate your obedience to God? lazy? active? What?

2.

Freed From the Consequences of Sin

Romans 5–6

Claim Your Story

When you are young, you do silly things. When I was a freshman in college, I decided to ask what seemed like a simple question: "God, what do you think of sin?" I asked this as I started off on a run in rural Pennsylvania. I got about a half mile before I collapsed in great pain. I crouched in a field with diarrhea; I vomited in a nearby farmer's shed; I was so faint I needed to lie down. I thought I would die—when only five minutes earlier I was feeling great. So I prayed another prayer: "God, please take your hand from me, I am seeing a glimpse of what you think of sin." I experienced in a visceral way the vileness of sin and felt firsthand in my limited human capacity the powerful revulsion God has for sin. I learned that day what Paul might describe as being "in Adam."

How do you understand sin? How would you say God sees sin? Do you think you understand sin the way God does? How so? Fortunately, God does not leave us "in Adam" but has reconciled us to himself "in Christ." The tyranny of sin and death have been crushed on the cross, and God's redemption has been extended to us through faith in Jesus Christ crucified. That is something worth taking time to contemplate. And to rejoice in.

Enter the Bible Story

Paul begins Chapter 5 with "therefore," which signals to the reader that he is drawing a conclusion based upon his previous argument. In this case, Paul has just explained that those who have faith in Christ are for-given of their sins and are declared righteous. This good news is not a "get out of jail free" card, wherein the individual continues life as before. For Paul, forgiveness opens the door to a new relationship with God, a rela-tionship characterized by peace and grace. With this new vista opened, our problems are recast as opportunities to develop our trust for and love of God. The term *problems* carries the idea of pressure, of being squeezed to the point of rupture. He speaks of the external problems faced by the Macedonian churches, especially their extreme poverty (2 Corinthians 8:2). None of these afflictions can separate us from God's love (Romans 8:35); and, though hard to imagine in the midst of suffering, all will seem light and momentary compared with the eternal glory that awaits believ-ers (2 Corinthians 4:17). To those who have watched their dreams die with the death of their child, or suffered the setback of unemployment, or walked through the valley of physical or mental illness, Paul validates their pain. But he is convinced that death, hardship, and disease do not have the final word.

Speaking of Hope

Several times in the first five verses Paul speaks of hope. He is not talking about the sort of emotion we have when we wish for a sunny day for our picnic or even the deep desire that the medical tests come back with good news. Paul emphasizes the firm conviction that God's ultimate plan for the renewed heaven and earth will be a reality. Paul declares that we can boast in this truth, that God will be glorified as God establishes God's reign forever. Moreover, this certainty develops deep within us as our character is shaped through steadfast trust in God's provisions. We boast with our lips that God will prevail, and we live out that conviction in our choices to endure whatever hardships come our way. A believer might be mocked for not following the latest "get rich quick" fad or might face derision from neighbors and coworkers for not bending the rules at work, but the scorn will ultimately prove groundless. Earlier, in Romans 1:16, Paul declares that he is not ashamed of the gospel. What could he be ashamed about? To the Corinthians, Paul explains that God's family is comprised not of the best and the brightest from the world's perspective. God does not recruit only the top students or the sports stars (see 1 Corinthians 1:26-31). God calls to everyone and all are welcome. This rag-tag bunch seems inauspicious, but their apparent lack of natural talent only serves to highlight the power of God. Since God does not evaluate us based on the world's yardstick, neither should we judge ourselves in this manner. We are the dwelling place of the Holy Spirit, and God's love overflows in our hearts.

Paul uses a familiar form of argument that if the lesser is true, how much truer is the greater. If God forgave us in Christ when we were actively fighting against God, how much truer it is that God saves us. If we are now reconciled to God in Christ, how much more confident we can be that our salvation is secure. Paul makes it plain that God accomplished our salvation while humanity was in active rebellion against God. We have trouble grasping this truth because we operate in a system that values meritocracy wherein individuals are judged on their performance. Secretly, we hear a whisper that we have to do something to merit salvation. We often think there really is something we should do even though we may accept Western culture's notion that humanity is fundamentally good at heart. But Paul's evaluation of humanity as thoroughly sinful undergirds his proclamation that it is only God's grace that reconciles us to God through Christ.

Adam and Christ

Why does Paul hold the conviction that humanity is sinful? He argues that all humans are like their first parent, Adam (5:12-14). Paul does not make a one-to-one comparison between Adam and Christ. Rather, his analogy is limited to the results of each one's singular act. Paul argues that the deed of each has ramifications for those who are part of their family. But the two deeds are not equal in value, for Christ brings life. The three key points of Paul's argument are (1) that humans can trace their lineage to the first man, Adam, who sinned, (2) that every person is gripped with sin, and (3) that every person faces the consequences of his or her sins, namely death. In some manner that Paul does not specify, Adam's sin resulted in death not just for himself, but for all subsequent humans. How is the effect of sin passed down through generations? Some suggest that it is passed along biologically. The idea of being present when your ancestors did something is found elsewhere in the New Testament in the argument in Hebrews 7:10, which states that Abraham gave a tenth of his wealth to Melchizedek, as did Levi, who was born generations later (for the Melchizedek story, see Genesis 14:18-20). Others, perhaps more accurately, argue that Adam represents all humanity, and as such, his sin was imputed to his descendants.

Across the Testaments

Genesis and Romans

The two Creation stories found in Genesis 1:26–3:24 begin with great promise and end with utter failure and despair. God declared that humankind, male and female, would be made in the image of God and would tend the lush garden created for them. Only one thing lay between them and utter happiness, one rule that must be obeyed. In the midst of the garden grew the tree of the knowledge of good and evil, whose fruit was forbidden. When the first couple took and ate the fruit, their lives changed forever. They saw both each other and God through eyes of fear and competition. For their deed, God cursed both the serpent who lied to them and the ground. Adam and Eve were banished far from the garden and from another tree that grew there, the tree of life. According to the apostle Paul, only in Christ can humanity be restored to the full relationship Adam and Eve enjoyed before they tasted the forbidden fruit (Romans 5:15).

Held in tension with the fact that Adam's sin affected us all is the truth that each person is also guilty of his or her own personal wrongdoings. As a consequence of Adam's sin, each person is unable to resist the draw of sin, and thus faces the punishment of death. We do not know how Adam's death infected everyone, but we do know that Christ's death is sufficient for everyone, because the gift is not like the transgression. The gift is more powerful. The greater the sin, the greater is the demonstration of God's grace. But is it fair to be found guilty for someone else's crime? Not in our court system. Does Paul argue for such an unjust scenario, with all humans paying the price for one man's sin? No, the courtroom analogy misses Paul's emphasis. Rather than a courtroom scene, a better picture might be of a geneticist's office. Together with Eve, Adam shaped his progeny. Along with hair and eye color, Adam passed along his flawed human nature that gravitates toward disobedience. Perhaps a better question would be, is it fair to profit from another person's deed? In this case, the deed is Christ's death on our behalf. It is God's gracious offer that we indeed share in eternal life through Christ's death, for all our failures have been erased from the books.

The Way to New Life

Paul explains in Chapter 6 that death provides the gateway to new life. Christ's death opens the way, and our own "death" to our former life in Adam brings forth the new life of service to God in Christ. Even more, we look forward to a resurrection like Christ's. As he did in Chapter 5, Paul uses the form of argument "if the former is true, then how much so the latter." In this case, he also adds a temporal dimension, so that what happened in the past will have an impact on what will be in the future. Paul connects our individual initiation into Christ's own work with our baptism, noting that we died (past) and are now alive (present and future) in Christ. With this union, Paul argues, we share in Christ's own work and reward. Our baptism into Christ is described as a burial to our old life; it signals a break with the past, with sin's power. As a result, just as Christ's death resulted in his resurrection, so too the result of our death in baptism is new life. In our case, we gain this new life in two stages. Currently we have life in the Spirit, and after the final judgment, we will have resurrected bodies fit for the new heaven and new earth (see 1 Corinthians 15:42-55).

About the Christian Faith

Romans and the Meaning of Baptism

The motive and moral power to live in true freedom (in other words, in "slavery to God") are found in that weaving of our life story together with the death and resurrection of the Messiah that happens in baptism. . . . If Jesus and his dying and rising are simply a great example, we remain without hope; who seriously thinks they can live up to that ideal in their own strength? But if the fact of the messianic events becomes part of our story through the event of baptism, and the prayer and faith that accompany it, and above all the gift of the holy Spirit . . . then we will indeed be able to make our own the victory of grace, to present our members, and our whole selves, as instruments of God's ongoing purposes.[1]

Grace and Sin

How do you feel when you get something good or valuable you don't deserve? Thankful? uncomfortable? beholden? Accepting God's free gift of salvation in Christ means that we also accept God's verdict of ourselves as sinful, but now forgiven, acquitted, and full of Christ's life. Paul addresses in Chapter 6 two possible misconceptions about God's grace and our sin. In the first case (Romans 6:1-14), Paul argues against the perception that God's gracious glory is celebrated the more we sin, because that gives God the opportunity to flaunt God's grace. Perhaps behind this reasoning is the benefaction system of the ancient world that promoted self-aggrandizement. A patron would look for opportunities to give his or her clients gifts so that they would be in greater debt to the giver. The poorer the client, the more generous the patron, and thus the greater honor bestowed. Paul insists that God's complete hatred of sin renders worthless such a parallel with the human system of patronage. He introduces the Mosaic law into the discussion in 6:14, which at first glance seems out of the blue. But if we realize that Paul is drawing a picture of salvation history with broad strokes, then we can appreciate that Paul contrasts the former system or realm of God's Mosaic law and the new realm of salvation in Christ. In both cases, God shows grace to God's people. The contrast, however, lies in the law's lack of power to effect change or destroy sin in humans. Said another way, Paul distinguishes between the present age, which has been dominated by the law and sin, and the new age inaugurated in Christ's death and resurrection—the age of the Spirit. Paul declares that the law is powerless against sin because the law relies on human energy to achieve it, but Paul has shown that humans "in Adam" are trapped in the power of sin. Christ broke the power of sin, which means that we are also free from the law's demands.

Grace and Law and the Life of Faith

In the second case (Romans 6:15-23), Paul speaks to the relationship between God's grace and the law as pertaining to sin. Paul reasons against the view that because God's grace does not come as a list of instructions God's grace must therefore offer no critique of sin (6:15). Grace does not mean that no standards of behavior exist or that righteousness now has no place. Indeed, Paul argues, grace allows for the achievement of righteous obedience. We have the promise that sin is powerless in our lives. Paul speaks of believers as slaves of righteousness, beholden to its bidding. Paul desires believers to "be who they are," to live out the promise of new life. Some refer to this as Paul's indicative/imperative: we are redeemed in Christ (fact/indicative) and so we must act in a way that demonstrates that truth (imperative). Others describe this as justification and sanctification. Two potential problems emerge if Paul's indicative/imperative is off-balance. First, we can slip into legalism. This happens because our behavior is seen to have no organic connection to our salvation, the idea captured in the term *justification*. Second, we can disregard any call to moral living. This occurs when we collapse the two, which usually minimizes our moral responsibilities.

So what exactly does a holy life devoted to righteousness look like? For many, the image is of an egotistical snob living the life of joyless drudgery. Nothing could be farther from the New Testament's picture. The holy life is one lived in the Holy Spirit. The fruit of such life is love, joy, peace, patience, kindness, goodness, faithfulness, gentleness, and self-control (Galatians 5:22-23). The holy life is one brimming with confidence that

God will ultimately make all things right and bring true justice to all of creation. The holy life is one that is content in the knowledge that God gives ultimate significance to his or her obedient acts. Such joy and freedom are ours in Christ!

The theme of Romans 6 is primarily about living out our Christian life here and now. But Paul also includes the promise that believers will enjoy eternal life (6:22-23). Sometimes we imagine that salvation is synonymous with life in heaven; that being saved means only that you go to heaven when you die. What a paltry vision that is. Our salvation includes both joy-filled, holy living now and resurrection life in the new heaven and new earth when God makes all things new. Paul explains this more fully in Romans 8; but here he notes that eternal life is in one sense the natural outcome of our holy life. Not because we have in any way *earned* eternal life, but rather because our holy life has prepared us for the resurrected life to come. An incomplete analogy might be to think of our current life as an athlete might think of the off season—a chance to hone skills and prepare for the real action. Or we might think of our days as similar to an engagement period, a time of preparation for the real deal—marriage. The best is yet to come, but as we await the consummation when all will be made right and sin's very presence will be banished, we can enjoy the opportunity of living free from sin's grasp, available to serve God wholeheartedly.

Live the Story

Although sin's stranglehold on our actions has been broken, we do not always behave as though this were true. Think about those you know who fail to recognize a new stage in their lives: newly married spouses who flirt with coworkers, middle-age weekend athletes who imagine themselves as they were in high school right before they pull a muscle. In a much more serious vein, Paul pleads with us to remember that we are not the same as we were before we placed our faith in Christ. The inevitability of sin has been broken and each believer is now free from its tyranny. Are you still living as though you are enslaved to your past? When we say "she is a slave of fashion" or "he is a slave to his office," we describe those who believe that their self-worth is based on physical appearance or achievement. Could someone say that about you? When we lament that we just could not help ourselves (in viewing pornography, for instance) or that we just did what everyone else does (in filing false income tax forms, for example), we fall victim to the lie that sin still has power over us. We deny the truth of our baptism—we died with Christ and we are dead to sin. When have you denied your baptism by your actions?

Paul notes in Romans 6:21 that sinful deeds bring shame to those who do them. Today, we tend to think in terms of innocence and guilt instead of shame and honor. Therefore we miss the corporate aspect to Paul's words, for shame implies a community that judges the behavior unacceptable. When I was about ten years old my grandmother pulled me aside at a public function and reminded me gently that "we Harrisons don't do such things." My behavior was unacceptable not just because it was wrong, but because it did not reflect well on my family. I cannot remember what I was doing that caught her attention, but her words drove home to me that my actions speak for more than just myself; they reflect on the family. In the same way, as Christians our behavior testifies to the great change effected in us through Christ. We are brand new people. Next time sin tempts you, imagine Paul leaning over to you, like a grandparent, saying, "we Christians don't do such things."

1. From N. T. Wright, "Romans," *New Interpreter's Bible*, Vol. X, p. 548.

3.

At Once Condemned and Acquitted

Romans 7–8

Claim Your Story

Have you ever felt paralyzed by guilt over a failure to love, obey, and resist evil? Have you ever felt complacent about God's forgiveness, imagining yourself not nearly as bad as the next guy? Guilt and forgiveness are two of the hardest realities to comprehend. So when our lives are touched by tragedy or evil, when we lose a job or a loved one, or experience the pain of our own failures, we cry as did Paul, "Who will deliver me?" (Romans 7:24). The answer is swift in coming: in Christ, believers are free, no longer bound to their sinfulness and this world's hopelessness (8:1). Our inheritance as coheirs with Christ is the promise of unending life with God, the hope of sharing eternity with fellow believers in Christ, and the conviction that even now the Holy Spirit seals our redemption.

Consider what it means to view all of your life, the good and the bad, from the perspective of God's promise of redemption.

Enter the Bible Story

Using logic, Paul draws on the legal codes surrounding marriage to explain the fact that believers in Christ must die to their old ways and live in the new life through Christ. He makes the obvious point that a dead person cannot be guilty of a crime nor fulfill a mandate. So, too, a marriage is possible only with both spouses living. In Romans 7:2-3, Paul uses the wife as the example, because among Gentiles at this time, a husband could only be accused of adultery if he had sexual relations with another married woman. He could have sex with prostitutes, freed women, or slaves without being accused of adultery. But in 7:4 the argument takes an unexpected turn. We would expect for the sake of continuity that Paul would argue that the law, our previous "spouse," died, freeing us to marry another. But Paul cannot say that, for the law is the eternal word of God. So he shifts the story such that we die and with us our marriage union. But then we come back to life through Christ. Our death ended the commitment to our previous spouse. Now we are free to marry again.

Notice how many times Paul draws conclusions from his statements of fact in 7:4-6, as Paul presents a "so that" clause. His logic is as follows: God does something that affects our right relationship with God, and therefore we are changed so that we behave in a different, holy manner. We died to the law, not to live as we please, but to be united to Christ. We are united with Christ not to indulge our passions, but so that we can experience the full life of holiness, bearing fragrant fruit pleasing to God. This is in marked contrast to the rotten fruit that resulted when we followed our own sinful desires. Our union with Christ brings promise of new life under the authority of the Holy Spirit. Paul's argument builds in crescendo, from establishing our death to the law and to our own self-centeredness, to proclaiming our new life in the Spirit, in union with Christ.

The Tension Between the Law and the Spirit

In Romans 6, Paul describes the law as "written," in contrast to the Spirit. This is a favorite distinction of his, to differentiate the letter written on stone (calling to mind the Ten Commandments) from the words of the Spirit written on our hearts (2 Corinthians 3). From this statement one might falsely assume that Paul has no regard whatsoever for the law. Yet he raises the question himself: is the law sin? And then he emphatically denies it, for the primary reason that it is holy, it comes from God, and it correctly establishes God's truth. The flaw is not in the law, but in the humans who are asked to keep the law. We cannot *keep* the law fully or completely, for sin is more powerful than our wills. According to Paul, the familiar saying "it's the thought that counts" just won't cut it. It is essential that the law be kept. That is why the law against coveting is so condemning. Often we can fool others (and even ourselves) by performing deeds of kindness, such as grocery shopping for a sick neighbor or loaning our lawn mower to a friend (or even cutting their lawn!). But we could do such things and harbor superior attitudes or selfish desires that they might repay us with even greater things. Paul admits that the tenth commandment, "Thou shalt not covet," exposes the futility of our puny strength against the might of sin.

Across the Testaments

Paul and the Law

The law is holy and good. Psalm 119 (an acrostic poem) expresses the great joy the Israelite enjoyed in meditating, practicing, and upholding God's law. Paul has no hesitation in confirming the law's holiness and goodness. But we must be clear about its purposes, especially now that Christ has come. First, not only does the law reveal what holiness looks like and what our holy God requires, but it also highlights that in ourselves we have no power to actually *do* all that is required. While the law included a system of sacrifices for forgiveness, this was a temporary solution to the overwhelming problem of sin (2 Corinthians 3:6-11). Second, Paul declares that the law shines a bright spotlight on that which would rather remain hidden in darkness.

Several questions arise in studying 7:7-25. First, Paul uses the first person throughout, leaving us to wonder if he is speaking autobiographically. Most commentators rightly reject this idea. Instead, Paul is speaking here as a representative of a group, much as he does in 1 Corinthians 13:1, when he declares, "If I speak in tongues of human beings and of angels but I don't have love, I'm a clanging gong or a clashing cymbal." We recognize that Paul intends for readers to put themselves in the verse, declaring that if anyone speaks without love, he or she only makes noise. A second question concerns the verb tenses used in this passage. In 7:7-12, Paul speaks in the past tense, most likely because he is looking back to the time when the law was introduced by Moses to Israel. In 7:13-25, however, Paul speaks in the present tense. This raises the question of whether he is speaking about the current life of believers, the current life of Jews, or the current life of any human. To answer this question brings up a third matter, namely whether anyone other than a believer can "desire to do good," (7:18) or "gladly agree with the Law" (7:22). One reading assumes that Paul is speaking to believers and unbelievers, with the corollary that this section refers to the Christian life. I suggest a better reading that understands Paul's argument directed at the problem of Jews under the law—for two reasons. First, a Jew can delight in God's law and can desire it; we see such sentiments peppered throughout the Old Testament, especially in the Psalms. I imagine Paul, too, recalls the love of God's law and the celebrations he participated in as he grew up in a Jewish home. But Paul also recognizes that forces more powerful than any human's own will effectively prevent the accomplishing of the law's demands. Second, Paul declares that this person who delights in God's law is also a "slave to sin's law" (7:25). Such a description hardly fits a Christian, who has died to the law and is now united to Christ. Believers are not prisoners of sin, but are slaves of righteousness.

Why is it that so many believers *feel* as though 7:13-25 accurately reflects their own life as a Christian? Perhaps it is because they try to do things under their own power and sheer strength of will. They have not completely accepted that sin is more powerful than their willpower and that sin's grip on them has been broken. Paul is *not* encouraging us to try harder—he is telling us, in the midst of our struggles, to turn to God.

No Condemnation for Those Who Are in Christ Jesus

In Chapter 8, Paul makes the joyous announcement that we have been rescued from sin. "So now there isn't any condemnation for those who are in Christ Jesus" (8:1), Paul declares. All judgments against believers are wiped clean in Christ. How is this possible? Paul offers two reasons. First, Jesus Christ is fully human; so he can represent every human before God. Second, Christ's resurrection has launched the age of the Spirit. Paul uses the term *law* to mean the Mosaic law and also the period, era, or system of reconciliation that God established. We live in a new

About the Scripture

Paul on the Spirit

"Paul more than any other NT writer links the concept of the Spirit given to indwell believers with living the Christian life. The Spirit is not only the power of God convincing believers of the truth of the gospel, not only promoting its preaching, but the Spirit is the power of new creation to those who have come to faith in Christ.... Christians who were formerly alienated from God have not simply been entered into the heavenly register of the redeemed; the Spirit indwells them and empowers them to live a life pleasing to God (Rom 8:1-4; 12:1; 1 Thess 4:1; to the Lord, 2 Cor 5:9; Eph 5:10). This life is described as being 'led by the Spirit' (Rom 8:14) or 'walking in the Spirit' (Rom 8:4; Gal 5:16, 25)."[1]

age governed by the Spirit. In this system, selfishness has no place. For example, we no longer judge as the world does, basing opinions on knowledge without love (1 Corinthians 8:1-3). Again, we do not allow social status or wealth to trump the genuine equality of worth shared by all people (1 Corinthians 1:26-29). Those who live in the realm of the self not only operate with a "me first" attitude, but also boast that "I did it all by myself." God is not thanked or even acknowledged as the source of all goodness and rightness. Said another way, just as we are not to live according to the law because we cannot meet its demands, so too we should not live under the power of our selfishness, our own mind, heart, and will that is damaged by sin. Instead, we embrace the new life open in the Spirit through Christ. You see, it is not enough that in Christ our souls go to heaven; that is not the picture Paul paints. He believes the Spirit is for the here and now, not just for the future.

Those who are in Christ are recognized by at least two characteristics: their lack of fear and their enduring familial ties. Paul might be drawing on a common picture in his day, the cowering slave and the confident child. Those who live in the realm of the self live with anxiety and dread that their good is never good enough—indeed they are correct about this!

Just as a slave has no control over his or her owner, so too human will is not able to gain the upper hand against sin. Beloved children, however, relax in their parent's presence, for they trust the compassion extended to them. Our adoption and inheritance is based on Christ's work and is lived out in the Spirit. But that does not mean that it is pain free. Paul declares that life in the Spirit as God's children will include suffering but will end in glory. And this glory is not ours alone but is glory and redemption for the whole world.

Suffering in the Present Age

Paul addresses the issue of suffering from the perspective of creation, which shares in the decay that characterizes this present age. The suffering is not pointless or random, but actually is leading toward a better end. It takes tremendous courage and faith to declare with Paul that our present sufferings rank as insignificant when compared to our future glory. Most all of us at some point will face a death or diagnosis that brings us right up against this statement. For me, it was my young adult sister's accidental death. Floundering in wave after wave of grief, it was hard (seemingly impossible) to withstand the onslaught. In those days, we hug tightly onto God's promise of a new heaven and earth much like a drowning person clings to a life preserver.

Paul speaks of the suffering as labor pains, which though painful in the end result in new life. Paul suggests that even creation itself is eager to have the resurrection of the sons and daughters of God take place. In 8:19, Paul says that creation waits eagerly for the children of God to be revealed. The word *revealed* is related to the term *apocalypse*, the final revelation of God at the last days, which will vindicate God's righteousness and set all things to right. To describe the creation's action as "eager longing" (NRSV), Paul uses a term found only here and in Philippians 1:20. Creation is portrayed as straining to see, standing on tiptoe to catch a view. The long-expected event or visitor is about to arrive, and onlookers crane their necks to catch the first glimpse.

Paul speaks about salvation as having a past, present, and future aspect to it. We were saved in Christ's death and resurrection. Paul speaks in the past tense in Ephesians 2:5-9: "God raised us up and seated us in the heavens with Christ Jesus." The historical events of Christ's cross and resurrection secure for believers an inheritance (Ephesians 1:14). Salvation has a present aspect, life in the Spirit, which Paul explains in contrast to a life in the flesh here in Romans 8. We are now in Christ, dead to sin and alive in the Spirit. The present age and the power of sin still wreak havoc throughout creation and especially in human lives. But this will not always be so, for Christ's tomb is empty and his body has been raised. Our salvation will be realized to the full at the final resurrection, when we receive our new bodies, imperishable, immortal, and when death is swallowed up in victory (1 Corinthians 15:53-54). How do we know this is so? How does a woman in labor know she will have a child? Has she seen who has been growing in her womb? No, but she has seen evidence from others, and everyone she knows has upon completion of pregnancy produced a girl or a boy. Christ's resurrection has given to each believer the firm hope that they too will be raised with a new body, because they are in Christ, and thus will be like him.

Sharing in Christ's Likeness

Paul writes that God works all things for good (8:28). People often say, "it will all work out" or "everything happens for a reason." This does not fully capture what Paul argues here, but it does hint at the reality that God is in control. Paul says something more profound, namely that God the Spirit pleads for the believer, and God the Father who shares the same will with the Son and Spirit works so that good comes out of circumstances that might seem hopeless. And what does that good look like? Paul declares that God will cause each of God's children to look like the Son. Each believer is on a journey that will end with their likeness to their "oldest brother" Jesus. We talk about family resemblances as we look at baby photos, exclaiming, "She looks just like her mother." "He has his grandfather's eyes." God has ordained that each believer will share not facial similarities with Jesus Christ, but Christ's holy character and righteousness.

Paul concludes that because it is God's will and wish that believers share life with Christ, it must also be the case that in Christ we enjoy all the bountiful blessings that God bestows. Perhaps one of the greatest of those blessings is our absolute confidence that God is on our side. That does not mean that God approves all *our* plans, ideas, or dreams. Rather, it means that sin cannot reclaim us, the law cannot repossess us, and our own sense of unworthiness cannot condemn us. Not only are we declared *not guilty*, not only are we promised to correspond to Christ's likeness, but we are also able to enjoy fully Christ's love in the midst of any sorrow, suffering, or pain. None of the heartache, none of the sleepless nights and agonizing days, none of the evil that seems to have the upper hand will be victorious in the end.

Live the Story

Take a moment and reflect on whether you *really* believe that you died to sin. Do you believe that with each temptation, you have the power in the Spirit to say NO to sin? Paul proclaims that you do. He is also a realist and recognizes that we will not always make the best decision, a point he addresses in the later chapters of Romans. Think back on a time when you clearly said NO to sin.

Have you allowed the wonderful news that your guilt has been paid for to sink deep within your heart? This is the promise of the gospel, which fits us for life in the present time and eternally. The metaphor of labor is a useful way to understand the impermanence and transitory nature of our life now. With a pregnancy, a mother can count on roughly nine months until she gives birth. Yet we are not nearly so sure of our lifespan here in this world, our present womb. Nonetheless, we can be confident that just as a mother will finish her pregnancy and give birth to new life, so also God will care for us as we grow into Christ's likeness, will keep us in and through our labor, and will welcome us home with open arms. The surety of our resurrection is also confirmed in the Spirit. Paul speaks of our prayers in suffering as groans. He assures us that the Spirit picks up where our own tongue has no more words to express our concerns, fears, and sorrows. If you know the tune to Charles Wesley's hymn "I Know That My Redeemer Lives," sing aloud this stanza:

I know that my Redeemer lives, and ever prays for me.
A token of His love He gives, a pledge of liberty.
Joyful in hope, my spirit soars to meet Thee from above.
Thy goodness thankfully adores; and sure I taste Thy love.
Thy love I soon expect to find, in all its depth and height;
To comprehend the eternal mind, and grasp the Infinite.

What about those believers who are asleep (Paul's euphemism for death) in Christ? The promised new heaven and new earth is yet still a promise; and so like us, believers who have died also wait. They wait in the love of God—for as Paul declares with absolute conviction: nothing can separate us from God's love, not death, and not life (8:38). Death does not and cannot strip away their garment of salvation, for they are clothed in Christ. They wait as members of Christ's body. Take a few moments to be quiet and enjoy the knowledge of God's lavish love for you through Christ.

---

1. From *Dictionary of Paul and His Letters*, edited by Gerald F. Hawthorne, Ralph P. Martin, and Daniel G. Reid (InterVarsity Press, 1993), p. 409.

4.

God Chooses All Who Call on God's Name

Romans 9–11

Claim Your Story

On March 23, 2000, Pope John Paul II spoke at Yad Veshem, Israel's Holocaust Museum, of reverent remembrance of the suffering Jews endured and the honor extended by the state of Israel to "Just Gentiles" who risked life and limb to aid their Jewish friends and neighbors. In these acts of compassion, the pope observed, we see "that not even in the darkest hour is every light extinguished. That is why the Psalms and the entire Bible, though well aware of the human capacity for evil, also proclaims that evil will not have the last word." Unfortunately, some Christians supported the Nazi ideology of racial supremacy (or remained silent), believing that the New Testament teaches contempt for Jews and Judaism. A close reading of Romans, Chapters 9 through 11, removes any notions that Paul might promote disdain for his people or for Judaism. Paul explains the Jewish people's position in God's salvation plan in light of Christ's work on the cross. His argument draws a picture of God as compassionate, merciful, and a keeper of promises. God extends his love to all people, freely. Can you embrace that love? Or do you feel that you must earn it? Paul challenges us to rest in God's great mercy.

Enter the Bible Story

Romans 8 ended with a eulogy to God about the greatness of our salvation. Paul praised the love of God expressed in the death and resurrection of Christ that no created thing can overcome. As he begins Chapter 9, Paul thinks about those of his own people who are not (yet) living in that love or do not recognize that love. In the next three chapters, Paul will say some seemingly harsh things about the Jewish position on the law vis-à-vis God's new revelation in Christ. These words have led some to say that Paul is anti-Semitic. When Paul wrote, however, the fledgling band of Jesus followers had no political power and was a minority in the synagogues. Paul extended the gospel message with a heart full of love and of sadness at the lack of positive response. He was speaking to his family, his fellow Jews. Paul's rebuke is that of a brother seeking to bring his siblings away from the brink of disaster. It seems an unwritten code that brothers and sisters can yell at each other, but if the same things were said by a neighbor to one of the siblings, one would rise up and defend the other. In a similar way, we must remember that Paul is a Jew, albeit one who follows Christ and who has been chosen by God to be an apostle to the Gentiles. In other words, Paul as a Jew had the credentials to speak pointedly to other Jews about what the Creator God was doing in their midst, that is, in Christ Jesus.

God's Faithfulness to Israel

Earlier, in Romans 3:1, Paul asked, "What's the advantage of being a Jew?" He did not answer the question extensively at that point, but he does so here in Romans 9. He lists the many benefits extended to Israel, including the promises, the covenants, the law, and the opportunity to worship the one true God. Paul also points out that from the Jews comes God's Messiah, Jesus Christ. Paul proclaims the concept of the Trinity that only later in the life of the church will be more explicitly expressed. Yet for all that advantage, most Jews do not embrace Jesus as Messiah. Romans 9:6 presupposes a challenge, namely that somehow because most Jews were not followers of Jesus, he was not the true Messiah. Paul declares, as he did in Chapter 3, that God is faithful, even if his people are not always so. God's character is at stake, Paul realizes, and it is imperative that Paul establish that God's plan cannot and will not be thwarted by any human action or accident of history. We can take great comfort in this truth, that no amount of suffering or persecution will destroy the church or defeat God's purpose for creation. As Jesus said to Peter, "I'll build my church on this rock. The gates of the underworld won't be able to stand against it" (Matthew 16:18). This promise holds on a personal level as well: each of us is to be conformed to the image of the Son, and nothing in heaven or earth can overturn that promise.

In Romans 9, Paul sets out to explain two things. First, not everyone who was born Jewish would be faithful to Jewish precepts; and second, God has always been in command of the future of God's people. Paul divides Jews into two groups, those who embraced the call of God on their lives and those who fell away. He will stress the latter in Romans 10 and return to a discussion of the former in Romans 11. Meanwhile, here in Chapter 9, Paul speaks of the two lines that come from Abraham, those born to Hagar and those born to Sarah, which Paul identifies as children of the promise. It is to this latter group that Paul looks when he shows that even within this assembly God's choice is sovereign and is not based on any person's deed or attitude. God is not indebted to any human, doesn't owe anyone favors, and can distribute full and fair justice. In the ancient world and so often today justice is bought. Paul declares that God cannot be corrupted, influenced, or in any way maneuvered by humans. God has established his salvation plan and will build up his people regardless of any historical contingencies. The last claim can sound to us despotic and capricious. Nothing could be farther from Paul's mind as he explains God's actions and character. Paul knows that God is merciful; indeed the quotation Paul cites in 9:15 is taken from the passage where God reveals himself and his glory to Moses. God *is* merciful and compassionate. In Africa, I learned a saying, "God is good, all the time; all the time, God is good." It is contrary to God's character to be arbitrary, fickle, erratic, or impulsive. No person has an inside track to getting favors from God, and none of us can convince God by our good deeds that God should or must grant us our wishes.

In Romans 9:19-23, Paul connects a potter's work shaping clay vessels to God's work forming a faithful people. He describes two types of jars, one used for ceremonial purposes and one used for common purposes. Paul is well aware that clay pots, if made unclean, are unable to be ritually cleansed, and so are tossed out onto the garbage heap. They were not like stone jars that could be washed in ritual baths and made clean again. Of course, Paul is not interested in pottery. He is interested in people—specifically, drawing an analogy between Jews and Gentiles. Most of Paul's first readers would assume that the pot made for special purposes is the Jew and the pot made for destruction is the Gentile. But Paul also speaks of pots made for mercy (9:23), pointing to those taken from both the Jews and the Gentiles, to make up the church. As he did in Romans 2, Paul speaks of a third category of people: believers made right by faith in Christ. Paul shows that Israel's own prophets declared this very truth.

God's Plan of Salvation

Zeal plus lack of knowledge can lead a person widely off track, and this is Paul's diagnosis of his fellow Jews. They are enthusiastic to serve God, but rather than submit to God's design of salvation through faith in Christ, they follow their own plan of salvation by doing the law. Our world is awash with similar sentiments. Many today are enthusiastic about God, extolling God's love and mercy. But they reject the claims of Christ as the mediator between God and humanity. They refuse to acknowledge sin's pervasive influence in the world and in each human heart, and they are uncomfortable with the reality that they need a Savior. So they try their best to do good things: to be kind, fair, honest, loving. They put a bandage on a gaping wound rather than submit to God's righteousness (10:3).

Israel's behavior rejects their own prophets' testimony to them. Twice Paul quotes Isaiah 28:16 that it is through faith that one is reconciled to God. Paul demonstrates that his gospel message is not innovative or contrary to God's promises; indeed, the gospel's emphasis on faith is a consistent theme thorough the teachings of Moses and the prophets. The emphasis on faith highlights two truths. First, God is the God of both Jew and Gentile, or in today's language, God is the God of all peoples, no matter their ethnic, racial, or national identity. The Trinity—Father, Son, and Holy Spirit—is the one true God. Second, it means that underneath the numerous dividing categories placed on people today, including social,

Across the Testaments

Paul and Isaiah

Isaiah's story of Israel's disobedience, subsequent exile, and eventual restoration resonated with Paul. Isaiah prophesied that not only would God redeem Israel from its oppression, but also Gentiles would join its numbers. Paul saw his own ministry to the Gentiles fitting with these promises but understood that his fellow Jews continued living in the earlier chapters of disobedience and exile.

religious, and political identifiers, humans share a common need and a common answer to that need. All need forgiveness, and all have access to forgiveness through faith in the faithfulness of Christ Jesus, shown in his death and resurrection.

No Distinction Between Jew and Greek

Paul raises a series of questions in Romans 10:14 that he answers in verses 18-19. To those who would say that salvation by faith in Christ has taken Israel by surprise and that they should therefore not be held accountable if they refuse to believe, Paul responds that God has indeed prepared his people to receive the good news. Through Isaiah and Moses, God explained that faith is the foundation of his relationship with his people. Again, God established that God reveals himself not only to Jews, but also to all the nations. Sadly, Isaiah also laments that many Jews even in his day rejected God's overtures. Some today use Romans 10:14 as a call to missions. It is true that God asks each believer to have an answer to the hope that they confess, and Christ instructs the church to go forth and make disciples of every nation, baptizing in the name of the Father, and the Son, and the Holy Spirit. However, Romans 10:14 has a more limited goal of declaring that Jews who reject the gospel are without excuse in terms of their failure to heed God's work in Christ. God is faithful to prepare the way for salvation, but God allows for each of us to choose disobedience.

In Romans 11, Paul anticipates several questions arising from his pronouncement that Israel was alerted to God's activities and was told that God desires faith, not deeds. He anticipates the idea that Israel has been rejected by God and dismisses the thought outright. First, he notes that throughout Israel's history, some followed God and others rejected God and turned to idols. Second, Paul declares that the Jews' mistake now in pursuing their own righteousness instead of faith in Christ does not rule out a change of heart later. Finally, Paul cautions his Gentile readers against any triumphalism or superior attitudes over against the Jews. Paul sketches out God's tactics, noting that the Gentiles' newfound relationship to God through Christ might spur his fellow Jews to look more closely at God's gift in Christ. Israel has shown a history of faithfulness that God will not ignore; in short, God will not withhold mercy.

The Scarlet Thread of God's Mercy

Throughout Romans 9–11, a scarlet thread of God's mercy has been woven. What does God's mercy look like? It is compassionate, generous, patient, extended to all people, and long-suffering. God's mercy cannot be bought or finagled; it is not extended for a moment then yanked away. Jesus revealed this mercy when he declared "Jerusalem, Jerusalem, you who kill the prophets and stone those sent to you! How often I have wanted to gather your people just as a hen gathers her chicks under her wings. But you didn't want that" (Luke 13:34; see also Matthew 23:37 and Luke 19:41).

Paul shows that God is consistent and compassionate in God's dealings with Israel and thus can be trusted in his work through Christ. Paul contrasts the remnant or "remaining group" (11:5) with those who resisted God's appeal (11:7). Paul expresses God's great kindness toward Israel, that despite their initial rejection of salvation by faith in Christ, God continues to extend the offer through God's grace (11:23). And not only to Israel, but to each person, God reaches out with the indescribable gift of grace. Psalm 103:11 describes it well, "as high as heaven is above the earth, that's how large God's faithful love is for those who honor him." Jesus looked up into a tree to call Zacchaeus and looked downward to the pros-

Across the Testaments

The Scarlet Thread of God's Mercy

The "scarlet thread" of mercy or redemption refers to the evidences throughout the Bible of blood and blood sacrifice as the means through which God brings about human redemption and reconciliation.

The metaphor of the scarlet thread (or sometimes crimson cord) most likely comes from the account in Joshua 2 of Rahab who risked her own life to save the Israelite spies and then saved herself and her family by leaving a "crimson cord" tied to her window as a sign. Another use of crimson or scarlet colored thread appears in the instructions for building the tabernacle and creating the environment for the ark and the vestments for the priest (see Exodus 25–28). The Israelites were asked to bring offerings, including "blue, purple, and crimson yarns and fine linen" (25:4, NRSV), which were then used to make the curtain that surrounded the ark, significant for many reasons, most especially for its *mercy seat.*

The idea of blood sacrifices appears in Scripture even earlier, however. In Genesis 4:4 we read that "the LORD looked favorably on Abel" and his offering of an animal sacrifice. Genesis 9:4 records God's prohibition to Noah against eating flesh with the lifeblood in it. Genesis 22 details the account of Abraham's near sacrifice of Isaac. In Exodus 12 we read about the institution of the first Passover and the account of marking the doorposts and lintels of the Israelite's houses with the blood of the lamb. Leviticus 17 details the system of sacrifice the Lord established. "For the life of the flesh is in the blood; and I have given it to you for making atonement for your lives on the altar; for, as life, it is the blood that makes atonement," the Lord instructed Moses (17:11, NRSV).

Beginning with the Gospels, we read accounts of Christ's sacrificial death on the cross, which is further recalled throughout the New Testament with references to Christ's sacrifice (see Romans 3:24-25, 5:9; 1 Corinthians 10:16; Galatians 6:14; Ephesians 1:7; 2:13; Colossians 1:20; Hebrews 9:12-14; 10:19; 12:24; 13:12-13, 20) and culminating in Revelation's praise of Jesus who "freed us from our sins by his blood" (1:5).

Woven throughout the pages of the Bible is the "scarlet thread of God's mercy."

trate blind beggar to offer him sight. He taught the Samaritan woman about true worship and the Jewish leader Nicodemus about true humility. Gentiles such as the Canaanite woman and the centurion received his grace, as did the apostle Peter's Jewish mother-in-law. No one today has traveled so far down the path of evil that God's right arm is too short to

About the Scripture

Tree Grafting

In Romans 11:17-24, Paul uses the analogy of grafting wild olive shoots into a cultivated olive tree to illustrate the argument he is making in Romans 9–11 regarding God's redemptive promise to Jews and Gentiles. Paul was counting on his hearers to be familiar with the process of cultivating olives. While olive trees are quite hearty and can grow to be hundreds of years old (some even surpassing a thousand years), they do not propagate themselves well through their own seeds and some varieties produce poor fruit on their own. Consequently, the ancient Greeks and Romans became skilled in the practice of grafting young shoots onto a mature tree to produce the choicest fruit. A small twig, called a "scion," would be taken from a (wild) variety of olive tree, trimmed at its base, and stripped of its leaves. Next a cut was made in the desired target tree where the wild twig was then inserted beneath the bark. The graft was stabilized by a seal made of clay or by a binding made of twine. The grafting bond happened where the inner barks of both the twig and the tree met, where the life of the stock flowed into the shoot.

bring back. Conversely, no one today has lived such an exemplary life that he or she need not humbly receive God's offer.

Having rightly presented God as actively desiring to reconcile all people through Christ, Paul wants us to realize that God does not act casually toward sin. Indeed, God will not tolerate it. First, Paul makes clear that God will judge all people and the entire world. Second, Paul warns against any presumptive attitudes on the Gentiles' part that assume God will never judge them as he has judged Israel. We Gentiles tend to display a common human reaction to good fortune, namely we assume that something intrinsic to ourselves brought us this luck and we feel superior to those who have hit bad times. While Paul acknowledges that Israel has stumbled because of their own waywardness, he also cautions the Gentiles to learn from Israel's example that God will not tolerate disobedience. The same standards apply to all, and all will be judged. The same God who will judge our neighbors' sin will also shine the light on our own deeds. And if our neighbors confess and repent, God will receive them. If we think that our church membership or our long-standing good deeds in the community allow us to look down our noses at those who have fallen, we should expect to be disappointed.

What will happen to Israel? Paul argues that Israel's resistance to the gospel actually works to spread the gospel. The Gentiles through faith in Christ receive the Holy Spirit and become members of God's family. Paul hopes that Jews, seeing the joy and peace through the Spirit enjoyed by Gentiles, will yearn with a jealous longing for the same thing (11:14). Paul also declares that "all Israel will be saved" (11:26). Paul looks forward to the day when his fellow Jews will receive their "deliverer" who comes to Zion and takes away their sins. This deliverer is none other than Christ Jesus. Israel's disobedience does not remove them from God's love; rather it provides the opportunity for God to show mercy to them even as God has to the Gentiles. In referring to "all Israel" Paul is speaking of Jews in a corporate sense. Similarly we might speak about the whole neighborhood coming to the picnic, or all the church coming to hear the guest preacher. We are not stating that every single person in the neighborhood showed up, or that every single member of the church attended. Rather we imply that a representative majority came.

In reflecting on God's tenacious love that pursues all people with God's mercy, Paul burst into song celebrating God's wisdom and grace. Sin is defeated not only for one group of people, but for all humankind. Mercy is given freely to all—what other response is proper but the one Paul models? With Paul each of us can sing—to God be the glory, great things he has done!

Live the Story

I thought my grandfather was one of the greatest men ever. He was always laughing, and he let me sit on his lap and steer his big truck around the block. So I was shocked to learn years after he died that while my father was growing up, he heard my grandfather refer to Jews as "Christ killers." The prejudice was deeply rooted, although it rarely came to the surface. Even today, deeply held prejudices against Jews, and against other groups, have engrained themselves into the very fabric of our lives. Paul's message forces each of us to examine our heart, to let the light of Christ expose and destroy such attitudes of superiority. And we can't stop there. It is not enough that we think rightly, we must also act in accordance with our convictions.

We can start with the church itself. An old joke talks about Saint Peter giving a tour of heaven showing the newcomers the many rooms in God's mansion. They pass various denominations in their rooms, and then Peter asks that the tour tiptoe past the final room. He explains that this group thinks they are the only ones here! We chuckle at the punch line, but we also know that it is true to some extent, not only within our particular denomination or church family but even within our own hearts. Do you think there are some believers who do not deserve to spend eternity with God? Are there some people you would just as soon God not extend the invitation to salvation? Might we be the persons someone else thinks undeserving of God's invitation to salvation? For what actions do you need forgiveness, and from whom? Ask God to open wider your heart and mind that God's forgiveness can flow in your own heart and overflow to others.

5.

A Community Shaped by Sacrificial Love

Romans 12–13

Claim Your Story

Can you recall a time when someone gave you a gift that you knew cost a great deal? Have you ever received hospitality from a stranger? Have you ever received a smile and a wave after you accidentally cut someone off in traffic? Years ago my husband and I were heading to an evening Bible study. We realized we were about to miss our exit and so quickly shifted lanes, cutting off the person behind us. The driver got very angry and began to "tailgate" us—that is, until it became clear to all of us that we were going to the same place! Once we arrived at our destination, the driver we cut off apologized for his anger, and we laughed about the whole thing. But we all learned the importance of Paul's command to bless—not curse—those who do you wrong. When have you caught yourself "cursing" those who trouble you? In what circumstances can you most easily think more highly of yourself than you ought? How have you repaid evil for evil?

Enter the Bible Story

Beginning in Romans 12, Paul points back to the mercies of God that he explained in Chapter 11, those extended to everyone, because everyone has been disobedient. This mercy, Paul urges, requires our response of faith and submission. Paul calls it "living sacrifice," which is an oxymoron, as every sacrifice is by definition dead. Recall that in Romans 6 Paul declared that we died to our old self in our baptism and we are raised to new life. Paul draws on that image again here. In mentioning our bodies, he communicates the Christian truth that we are not souls trapped in matter; God made Creation good and our bodies will be redeemed in the Resurrection. Jesus calls us to take up our "cross daily, and follow me" (Luke 9:23). In other words, we are called to die daily to self and to live for God. We commit each day to God, open our hearts to God's leading, and rehearse in our minds God's promises. When we get bad news about our children, our job, or a friend's health, we breathe a prayer of hope that God will be glorified in the midst of the sorrow. When we fail to act kindly to our friend or coworker, we ask forgiveness and then accept that God *really* has forgiven us (so we can forgive ourselves).

A Living Sacrifice

Paul presents the believer as a priest serving in God's sanctuary. The image he offers is one in which each believer offers a sacrifice to God, a sacrifice of him or herself. Then having died to sin, we walk in new life. Each day, we lay down our own agenda, our own desires, and submit to God's will and plan. So what is that plan? God has provided a number of ways that believers can understand and then do God's will. First, we have the Holy Spirit who guides and directs us. Second, we have Christ who intercedes for us. Third, we always have an open door to the throne room of grace where in Christ we may petition the Father. Fourth, we have God's Word, the Bible, which reveals God's character and Person, as well as expectations for and promises to believers. Fifth, we have the church, our believing brothers and sisters, who can pray with us, teach and admonish us, and encourage us.

Paul cautions us that old habits of heart and mind die slowly, and we are in danger of falling back into old ways of thinking and behaving. What are the patterns of this world? From the first three chapters of Romans we see one pattern: humanity's selfish rejection of God's goodness and adoption of an attitude of thanklessness and arrogance. Romans 5 suggests another pattern: the failure to appreciate the attractive yet harmful nature of sin and its pervasive hold on the human heart and mind. In the remaining chapters, we observe yet another pattern: self-righteousness toward God's revelation and self-promotion over against those groups that differ from us. According to Paul's argument in Romans, such self-centered patterns of thought and deed are simply contrary to God's will.

So that everyone is very clear about his message, Paul comes straight to the point: don't sing your own praises and don't believe your own press. Jesus said it in a similar way: "Love your neighbor as yourself" (Luke 10:27) and "Treat people in the same way that you want people to treat you" (Matthew 7:12). All we are and all we do are gifts of God's grace. God calls and God equips, and then God blesses and grows the fruit of our labor. We cannot take the credit for anything other than our obedience—and even that is a gift of the Holy Spirit. Today, our individualism resists this teaching as unnecessary self-belittlement. But believers know better; we understand the depths of sin's wickedness and the heights of human folly when self is on the heart's throne. Paul message is one of freedom, freedom from having to produce, having to succeed, having to meet some (arbitrary) measure before receiving acceptance.

The Body of Christ

Christians through the centuries have been tempted to see their spiritual development in individualistic terms. By speaking about the unity of the different members of Christ's body directly after asking believers to be living sacrifices, Paul emphasizes that transformation occurs in community. Paul explains that God has measured out a portion of faith, meaning that God has declared how we are to measure or evaluate ourselves: not by our own acts, but according to faith. The measure of our salvation is "not something you did that you can be proud of" (Ephesians 2:9). This common gift of grace is granted to all believers and grounds our unity. But we also differ from each other in terms of our specific gifts and responsibilities within the body of Christ. God equips each believer to function within the body or Christ, the church.

Each of us has been gifted with abilities, talents, and opportunities to grow personally in our understanding of God and to serve other believers and the world. Paul argues that each of us has been given a gift "in proportion to your faith." He is not simply listing gifts of the Spirit, but exhorting believers to use their gifts diligently. Moreover, the expression of these gifts must correspond with the gospel, the faith handed down by the apostles. This portion of faith is sufficient for each one of us to accomplish our responsibilities. We cannot say we have a gift but not enough grace to live out that gifting, for God has equipped us fully. Those of us who are teachers, for example, cannot say to God that we were unable to live out our gifting because we just did not have enough grace to get us through our preparation for teaching, or not enough faith to help us with troubling students, administration, or coworkers. We learn from stories in the Old Testament that God does not give in to our whining; God did not budge when Moses said he could not speak for God to Israel (Exodus 3:10–4:17) and God did not have a change of heart when Jonah refused to obey (Jonah 1:1-3; 3:1-3; 4:1-4, 9-11). God has fully equipped each believer for the jobs that she or he will do for the body of Christ.

The Body of Christ, Gifted for Action

Having described the different gifts that make up the one body, Paul further explains how those gifts are to function: in love. In 1 Corinthians 12–14, Paul discusses gifts of the Spirit; and in the midst of his teaching, he pauses to pronounce the central importance of love governing all of the believers' actions. The Greek text of Romans 12:9-13 is one long sentence with many phrases. The key thought that governs all the phrases is that love must not be hypocritical; our love must be sincere. What does sincere love look like? It means we treat other believers as members of our own family, including opening our home to them. It means cultivating friendships with those who in society's eyes do not have high status or wealth. It means showing respect to all, enthusiastically championing the truth of the gospel, and fervently praying that God's will be done in your heart, in your church, and in the world. Paul orders us to bless those who persecute us. This is not a suggestion but a command to imitate our Lord who on the cross prayed that God the Father would forgive those who persecuted him (Luke 23:34). Paul also commands us not to think too highly of ourselves. From these important commands come specific consequences. If we *really* are blessing those who persecute us, then we must not repay anyone evil for evil. If we *really* are keeping a check on our egos, we can associate freely with those who in the world's eye have low worth. If we honestly consider ourselves as one among many, then we have a better opportunity to live at peace with all around us.

Paul closes by quoting two verses from the Old Testament that demonstrate God's requirements for living honestly and lovingly in community and God's determination to judge all humankind fairly in God's time. We are free to love, leaving the judgment to God. Paul knows it is hard to stay angry at someone after he or she shares a meal with you. Partaking together usually leads to conversation and sharing, the building blocks of relationship. By showing genuine compassion and charity, we allow the love of Christ to overflow into another's life.

Why is revenge bad? Because it begins at the wrong place—it starts with an offended ego. It develops with faulty knowledge, for what human can know fully another person's heart? It ends with escalating violence and fractured communities. Paul asks us to rest in God's justice. God knows the whole story and will not ignore those who sin against another. Our focus should be on caring for those who have determined to dislike us. In this way we mirror God's behavior toward us. As Paul described in Romans 5:8, while we were still sinners, enemies of God, Christ died for us. Who knows, perhaps extending Christ's compassion might cause this "enemy" to become a friend.

The Body of Christ and the Body Politic

It is perhaps no accident that Paul speaks of submitting to government authority when writing to the Romans. More than any other Christian community, the Roman believers faced the full blast of imperial propaganda and military might. Paul provided a lens through which they could view their position as a small minority group who could not offer worship in the imperial cult. They could be solid members of society by following those rules that did not demand idolatry. While their witness of love and charity had an impact on their witness to neighbors, their stand against emperor worship took its toll. After the great fire in Rome that

About the Scripture

Romans and Saint Augustine

According to his own account in his *Confessions*, the early church father, Augustine, was converted to the Christian faith after reading a portion of Romans 13. During a time of intense personal crisis, Augustine heard what he believed to be a child's voice from a house nearby, chanting over and over the words: "Take up and read." Convinced the very voice of God was instructing him to read the first thing he put his hands on, Augustine returned to his home and picked up the book he had left laid open. The book was Romans and Augustine's eyes fell upon 13:13-14: "Let's behave appropriately as people who live in the day, not in partying and getting drunk, not in sleeping around and obscene behavior, not in fighting and obsession. Instead, dress yourself with the Lord Jesus Christ and don't plan to indulge your selfish desires." As a result of his inspired reading of Paul's letter, Augustine became one of the most influential theologians in the history of Western Christianity.

raged for six days and destroyed three quarters of the city, Christians were blamed for the disaster. Nero hoisted them up on poles and set them aflame, jeering that they were street lamps. Most Romans were aghast at such cruelty and, along with Paul, would not have expected Christians to respect or accept such depraved behavior. Yet in matters of taxes and other laws that serve to keep the public peace, Paul insists that believers yield to government authority.

Paul's message begs a question: Why do we work so hard to avoid submitting to authorities? We "help" other drivers not get caught speeding by flashing our lights to warn them of police officers ahead of them. We lie about our children's ages to get them into a movie more cheaply. Paul knows that this sort of behavior is a recipe for disaster, both on a personal and a social level. At the social level, Roman government generally promoted fair laws and provided justice to those who had been wronged by thieves or treachery. What the ancient world feared most was anarchy and chaos. In those circumstances, people died, homes were destroyed, and despots emerged who trampled all in their path. Government kept anarchy at bay and established laws rather than allow for a tyrant's impulsive whim to rule the day. So for social stability, believers should support their government. Yet Paul also stresses that our conscience requires that we follow the rules. In paying taxes, we show respect and honor to those whose job it is to preserve the peace.

Notice what Paul is not saying. He is not advocating blind obedience to all decisions or policies. Nor is he imagining a representative democracy that promotes citizen participation and nonviolent civil disobedience. Those who were being governed had no acceptable means to challenge government policies that were deemed unfair or unwise. As citizens of a democracy, we have great responsibility to engage in political conversation and shape our government, even as we submit to existing laws and the system in place to change laws or policies deemed unjust.

After treating a believer's response to government, Paul points to a higher law, the one established by God. These commands take precedence over any human orders. Following Jesus' teachings, Paul declares that all commandments are summed up in loving others as yourself. We are all under the obligation to actively look for opportunities to be gracious, forgiving, and generous. Our desires turn outward as we think of ways we can bless those around us. Today we hear the caution that we have to take time for ourselves. This implies that we have a finite reservoir of love and that we drain ourselves as we love others. This is not Paul's model. He argues that the love we share with others has its origin in Christ's love for us and takes its replenishment from the indwelling Holy Spirit. The love of which Paul speaks is not an emotion or feeling; it is a commitment of the will to honor others above yourself. It is a pledge to refuse to sin, to draw a line against taking what is not yours, to guard others' reputation instead of stealing their good name. Believers never need a respite from this sort of love.

Paul began Romans 13 with a narrow focus on government, the human institution that seeks to regulate social interaction. He then spoke of the believer's obligation to follow not only human laws but God's law. Both of these instructions focus on our current situation. In the last section of this chapter, Paul reminds us that governments and social obligations are temporary, a necessary part of the present age. But soon God will complete our salvation and present us with our resurrected body fit for

Across the Testaments

God's Way

God desires a relationship with God's people and has made a way through Christ's faithfulness and our faith in God. Moreover, the commandments given to Israel at the very beginning of the biblical narrative prepare the way for Christ's redemptive work. In Leviticus 19:18, Moses speaks God's words to the people, "Love your neighbor as yourself; I am the LORD" (NRSV). In Deuteronomy 5:6-7, Moses delivers a crucial set of God's commandments to the people, including, "you shall have no other gods before me" (NRSV). Later, Jesus highlights both the Leviticus decree and the mandate to worship the one true God by connecting them in his own teaching. He announces that upon these two commands hang all the other commandments (Matthew 22:34-40; Mark12:28-34; Luke 10:25-28). Christ fulfilled both of these laws fully; and as believers, we too have satisfied them, for we are *in Christ*. In response to that good news, we are called to demonstrate that truth in our lives each day. We are called to love. That is and has always been God's way.

eternal life in the renewed heaven and earth. We do not know how soon this will happen, but each of us must be prepared to greet our returning Lord and Savior. Vibrant word pictures serve to enhance our imagination, as Paul explains that while the present age is darkness, Christ's light will soon dawn. Twice Paul asks us to put on what is ours in Christ. He asks that we put on weapons of light and put on or dress ourselves with Christ. In 2 Corinthians 6:6-7, Paul describes his own ministry using similar Greek terms, speaking both of love that does not pretend (Romans 12:9) and of weapons of light (righteousness) (13:12). The weapons of light shine God's truth into the darkness of sin that characterizes the present evil age. As we put on Christ, we declare ourselves to be people of God, in much the same way that shoulder pads or a stethoscope identifies a football player or a doctor.

Live the Story

"The clothes make the man (or woman)," so the saying goes. Children take great delight in dressing as their favorite super hero, princess, or sports idol. Though clothing can hide the truth or manipulate perception, our clothes can also remind us to act in line with the message they send. Dressing formally for a family member's graduation signals respect for his or her accomplishments. Dressing casually for a picnic indicates willingness to play on the swings with the children. Clothing ourselves with Christ speaks to the wider community that our identity is fundamentally as a follower of Jesus Christ. Moreover, putting on Christ each and every day reminds us of our worth as a child of God and that our focus should be on glorying God.

If we connect the image of clothing our bodies with Christ to the injunction to present our bodies as living sacrifices, we see how important it is that our confession of faith be matched by our actions. To continue with the clothing imagery, we have all seen people dress inappropriately for an occasion. Some are too sloppy, disrespecting their host. Some are too risqué, drawing sexual attention to themselves. Some are too flashy and flamboyant, setting themselves arrogantly above others. In the same way, if as believers we engage in sloppy work habits, we cheat our employer; if we indulge in sexual promiscuity (flirting, porn, fornication), we sin against our spouse, against our own body, and against our Lord with whom we are united by faith (1 Corinthians 6:12-17). If we promote ourselves over against others, we divide the body of Christ and make a mockery of its unity. As the high priest wore special garments when performing sacrifices to God, so too our garment (Christ) reminds us of our holy occupation—to live faithfully and serve charitably.

How do you insure that your public deeds, seen by your family, coworkers, and fellow believers, are consistent with your professed faith? How can you make a concerted effort each morning to "clothe" yourself with Christ? What might you do to remember during your day that you are in fact clothed with Christ?

6.

God's Welcome, Our Response

Romans 14–16

Claim Your Story

She was naturally hospitable: a ready smile, a quick wit, and the intuition to pick up my moods. She appreciated me for who I was, not what she wanted me to become. She lived out our biblical text with her attitude of service and her refusal to judge on the nonessentials. She was my lifeline in my new home away from home: Kenya. Remember your first day in a new high school, college, neighborhood, or job? Were there people who extended real friendship, who enjoyed your quirkiness and did not try to change you into their clone? How about in your church, how did you first experience God's welcome from the congregation? Are you actively welcoming new members yourself now? Do you delight in those who have different opinions from your own? God's family is as varied as the world's cuisines, languages, styles of dress, music, and so much more. But rather than celebrate the variety, we desire conformity and sameness. It makes us feel secure and in control, but such security is an illusion. When we embrace difference, we remember that we are not perfect and all knowing. Our differences serve to make more pronounced our unity in Christ. Who will you welcome this week? Whose differences will you embrace as revealing to you the greatness of God's design?

Enter the Bible Story

The Christian Life: Walking in Love

Paul recognizes that the church is a diverse gathering, a place where we bring our baggage, our assumptions, our experiences, and our prejudices. We are not all at the same point in our spiritual journey, and we each grow in our faith at different paces. This unevenness creates tension as differences are elevated to the level of moral imperative, causing us on occasion to pass judgment upon each other. Paul speaks specifically to the Roman church about the issues raised because of different eating habits. Why would this be a concern? In our culture most of us eat meat every day; it is cheap, readily available, and a good source of protein. But in Paul's day, almost no one had money to purchase meat for everyday meals. Meat was mainly associated with religious festivals. Both Jews and Gentiles would bring an animal to their respective temple to slaughter it and then have a celebration. Behind Paul's concern about meat and wine is pagan idolatry. Jews in Rome would only eat meat slaughtered in a kosher manner. They did not offer sacrifices in their synagogues and were probably too poor to buy meat except on rare occasions. Most Roman Gentiles probably had meat only after it had been sacrificed to the gods. Thus, a Jewish believer might reject any meat because he or she could never be sure it was slaughtered properly. And Gentile believers had trouble eating meat because it brought back so many memories of their former life of idolatry. Paul argues that meat sold in the market, apart from any pagan worship setting, is acceptable to eat (Romans 14:14), but he also admits that not everyone can live in that freedom.

Another issue revolves around views about sacred days. Some believers set aside the Jewish sabbath as a day of rest and perhaps kept certain Jewish festivals as well. Paul talks about returning to Jerusalem to celebrate Pentecost, for example (Acts 20:16). Others only see the Lord's Day as sacred. Each person can back up his or her stance with Scripture and church precedence. Neither position could be classified as sinful. Christian freedom is the key, for we are responsible to the Lord for our decisions.

We are not accountable for our brothers' and sisters' personal decisions on these matters.

It is crucial to realize that Paul is not talking about looking the other way when sinful behaviors are going on. He is speaking only about those practices that are neutral in terms of faith but that can create passionate responses. Today we don't worry about meat sacrificed to idols, but we do face situations that cause division. For example, some believers have no trouble including wine with a meal; others deeply distrust the consumption of any alcohol. Paul would ask those who are comfortable with drinking alcohol to refrain from drinking when those who are opposed to it are present. And those uncomfortable with the use of alcohol must acknowledge that its use is acceptable in the broad sense, even if they are not comfortable drinking. Neither is instructed to "convert" the other. Another example is worship style. Some disdain organ music as outdated and others can't imagine a church service without its music. Probably these two groups worship at separate churches (or different services of the same church), which is fine. What would not be good is for either of them to judge the other as inferior in worship or less passionate for God. The list could go on, including parenting styles, best marriage practices, and attention to environmental issues. Paul's counsel is that Christians not make personal preferences into law.

The Christian Life: Accountable to God

Paul reminds us that we will all give an account to God for our actions. At first glance, this seems at odds with Paul's earlier statements that our works count for nothing. But the circumstances of the two statements are quite different. In earlier chapters, he was at pains to explain that our relationship with God begins and ends with faith in Christ. We are brought into relationship by our faith in the faithfulness of Christ. Our relationship is sustained by walking by faith, not by sight (2 Corinthians 5:7). And our relationship will culminate when our faith and hope have been realized in the new heaven and earth. Here in Chapter 14, Paul addresses our responsibilities as God's children to obey God's charges and submit to

God's will. Our disobedience will not result in lost salvation, but it will be judged at the Last Judgment (2 Corinthians 5:10). Paul speaks to the Corinthians about Christ judging his ministry (1 Corinthians 4:1-5) and the context is similar to his remarks to the Romans. The Corinthian church was evaluating Paul and finding him lacking in certain areas. They wanted flashy presentations and clever speaking skills. Paul declares that he does not even judge himself, which does not make him innocent. It is the Lord who will judge. Paul is to be obedient to the call placed on his life—to be a faithful apostle to the Gentiles. We are to use our gifts for God's glory and for the benefit of the church and the world. We are to follow faithfully the precepts established for all believers, avoiding sin and actively pursuing love.

In Romans 14:17, Paul speaks about the kingdom of God, a phrase familiar in Jesus' teachings but rarely used in Paul's letters. Jews, however, would be very familiar with such language. Indeed, many misunderstood Jesus' ministry as a political movement to establish a Jewish nation free from Roman oppression. Yet Jesus maintained that his kingdom was not of this world, meaning that it did not operate as human empires did. Peaceful persuasion, not violent domination governs interactions. Social outcasts (Mark 10:23-25), children (Luke 18:16), those crippled with illness and disease (Luke 14:15-24) are welcome in God's kingdom. Those who recognize its value give up all to enter the kingdom (Matthew 13:44-46) and those who only give lip service to it will fail to be admitted (Matthew 7:21). The kingdom of God includes God's reign over his people. Our response as the community of believers is not to identify (and segregate) ourselves based on nonessentials and personal preferences, but rather to unite through the love, peace, and joy that is ours in the Spirit. When each of us is looking not to each other but to the Lord, our priorities sort themselves out. Just as we trip and stumble if we are not paying attention to where we are going, so too if we lose our focus on our Savior, we easily fall into criticism and judgmental attitudes. What distractions tempt you to take your eyes off the Lord? What personal preferences have you elevated to the status of "gospel truth"?

The Christian Life: Patience and Peace Over Power and Politics

Paul turns in Romans 15 to speak directly to the responsibilities of those who are powerful over against those who are not. In the previous chapter, Paul identified the "weak" as those who did not eat meat out of personal reservations as to its possible sinful connections. In this chapter he does not use the term *weak* but rather speaks of those who do not have power. Who are these people, and who are those who are powerful? He may be speaking in terms of their maturity in the faith; the powerful understand (as does Paul) that particular food, drink, or days of the week do not draw one closer to God. It is also possible that he is thinking of social status. Those who were comfortable eating meat previously sacrificed to idols probably had enough surplus money on occasion to purchase meat at the market. They enjoyed meat in contexts other than pagan festivals. To these wealthier believers, meat was not inherently connected with idolatry. Thus, their convictions that meat could be acceptable in some contexts were directly related to their social status. Oftentimes we imagine it is our superior intellect or great reservoir of faith that provides insight, but in actuality it is merely our own experiences and chance occurrences that shape our thinking. Rather than hoard their resources and influence, Paul demands that those with power use it for the betterment of the community.

About the Christian Faith

Paul and Rome

Paul wrote his letter to the church in Rome (mid-50s A.D.) while in Corinth, just before he was to return to Jerusalem with a collection for "the poor among God's people" there (Romans 15:26). He had yet to visit the city of Rome. When he did reach Rome, ironically it was as a prisoner under house arrest (Acts 28:16). According to apocryphal texts such as the Acts of Paul, the apostle's eventual martyrdom took place in Rome during the reign of the emperor Nero. Today the Basilica of St. Paul Outside the Walls in Rome stands upon the site believed to be Paul's burial place.

Because the issues defined as weakness have nothing to do with sinful behaviors, Paul urges the powerful to bear with or be patient with those with dissimilar views. Notice that the powerful are not asked to *teach* or to *change the behavior* of their fellow believers. The powerful are to focus on unity among believers, and this means to submit their own preferences to the larger group. Our example is Jesus, who as God's Son received the insults that are hurled against God by unbelievers. The author of Hebrews similarly remarks that Jesus ignored and even scorned the shame of the cross, knowing that his faithful obedience would bring redemption (Hebrews 12:2). Paul brings up the issue of insults, shame, and honor because the powerful were accustomed to being treated with deference. Their power must now be used in service to Christ. So too those who have a deeper understanding of our freedom in Christ must make it their aim to imitate Christ's attitude of service. Do you find yourself getting upset when others disagree with you about the style of music or the order of worship? Do you withdraw from fellowship if your ideas for a church program or the renovation of the church building are not approved? Can you accept as your spiritual equals those who disagree with you on issues of church polity, biblical interpretation, or even politics?

Paul reminds the Romans that in God's salvation plan we are all saved by God's grace. Christ welcomes us into the family, and we must do likewise for others. The greatest show of godly hospitality is the welcoming of Gentiles into the people of God through faith in Christ. To make his point, Paul cites several Old Testament passages that mention Gentiles. He does this for several reasons. First, Paul has already spent several chapters in his letter to the Romans establishing that the law cannot save because it cannot overcome sin. We have died to sin by sharing in Christ's death not by following the law. In short, our new life is based solely on God's mercy—a gracious gift extended to Jew *and* Gentile alike. Second, it is likely that the weak/strong division has a strong component of racial division. More Jewish believers than Gentiles probably abstained from meat and rested on the sabbath. Yet in Romans 11, Paul alluded to tensions between the two groups when he warned Gentiles not to become

Across the Testaments

God's Glory

Paul quotes Isaiah 45:23, which prophesies that all people will pay tribute to the Lord God. This promise blesses the believers' ears, for we long to have God glorified by all. We have no fears of being rejected by God, only the desire to hear Jesus praise our faithful service. But this word from Isaiah is also a warning to those who do not believe. Their defiance, neglect, or agnostic attitude toward God will be brought to account on the Last Day and they will acknowledge God's glory.

proud at the Jews' temporary hardening of heart. Third, Paul reiterates that God's plan from the beginning was to include Gentiles as members of God's family through faith in Christ, a plan that highlighted God's great mercy and faithfulness to God's promises. This signals for Paul that the restoration of all things promised in Isaiah has begun. Paul is overcome with gratitude and breaks into a short prayer for God's great blessings to shower upon them. He describes God as the God of hope, emphasizing that our salvation is sure. He asks that the joy and peace that is ours in Christ would spill over onto others as we grow in our faith. The Holy Spirit will guard our hearts and encourage our trust that God will accomplish our ultimate redemption and resurrection.

Plans and Instructions

As Paul closes his letter to the Romans, he assures them that he has utmost confidence in them. Remember, he has not yet met them and does not want them to think that he is arrogantly assuming they *need* his advice. Rather he explains that his letter was written out of a desire to serve them and to be faithful to God's calling on his life as an apostle to the Gentiles. He realizes that some of what he said might have been hard to hear, although he does not say what points specifically. His generalization allows us to pause a moment and reflect back on the entire letter. What was hard for you to hear? How is the Holy Spirit challenging you to trust God more in all areas of your life?

Paul spends a bit of time explaining his ministry in the regions around the Aegean Sea and his desire to get to Rome. Little did he know that his yearning would be accomplished while chained to a Roman soldier! He planned to visit Rome on his way to Spain, perhaps even enjoying the Roman believers' prayer and financial support. We cannot say for certain whether Paul reached Spain, but church tradition says that after his imprisonment noted in Acts 28, he was released and made it to Spain before being re-arrested and executed under Nero. How often in our own lives have we planned for something, only to have God supervene and plot an entirely different course? We look at what seems to be the best, easiest, and safest course to get the job we want or to live in the city we desire. Then circumstances occur that throw all our plans into the air, and we notice that God is orchestrating our destiny. Paul finally did get to Rome. Luke tells us that when the believers came out of the city to greet him, Paul "gave thanks to God and was encouraged" (Acts 28:15). Can we also be thankful that God is working God's will in our lives and might even disrupt our plans so that God will get the glory and we will see God's hand in our lives?

Live the Story

You have just completed the reading of one of the most important books in the New Testament. You have also just read a deep love letter to a church from a man who was a pastor at heart. As you reflect back on the various phrases you can remember or the key themes that caught your attention, consider how much of Paul's letter has shaped your thinking as a Christian. What of Paul's many admonitions throughout his letter do you need to heed? For instance, Paul admonishes Christians not to judge each other. One way to prevent a judgmental attitude is to get to know the persons whom you are criticizing. Another way is to pray for them, that God will work in their lives and bless them. A third way is to be in honest prayer with God about your own life. Jesus cautions us to remove the log from our own eye before attempting to help another remove the splinter in his or her eye (Matthew 7:5). In the Letter to the Romans, Paul shows God's offer of freedom in Christ, freedom from drawing our self-worth from comparisons with others, freedom to love and serve without thinking of what we will gain in return, freedom with fellow believers to appreciate how vast is God's love and care for his children. How will you use this freedom in Christ to serve others in your family? your congregation? your community?

Paul describes his own ministry as an apostle, making clear that he boasts only in what God has done in and through him. It is not always easy to understand where our acts of obedience fit into our confession that everything good we do is from God. Paul describes our behavior with phrases like "renewing your mind" or "submitting your will." These suggest that our obedient submission to God is our "part" of the journey, saying with Christ, "not my will but your will must be done" (Luke 22:42). It is for God to direct, enable, and bless the work (Ephesians 2:10). What does compel you toward obedience? Consider God's all-sufficient grace, amazing love, great faithfulness, and constant mercy, described so elegantly in Paul's letter. How do those phrases characterize your faith? If they do not characterize your faith in some way, then how might you address that deficiency?

With our salvation secure in Christ, our present hours sheltered by the Holy Spirit, and our final home established by our God the Father, we do well to join Paul in exalting our God with these words, "All things are from him and through him and for him. May the glory be to him forever. Amen" (Romans 11:36).

Leader Guide

People often view the Bible as a maze of obscure people, places, and events from centuries ago and struggle to relate it to their daily lives. IMMERSION invites us to experience the Bible as a record of God's loving revelation to humankind. These studies recognize our emotional, spiritual, and intellectual needs and welcome us into the Bible story and into deeper faith.

As leader of an IMMERSION group, you will help participants to encounter the Word of God and the God of the Word that will lead to new creation in Christ. You do not have to be an expert to lead; in fact, you will participate with your group in listening to and applying God's life-transforming Word to your lives. You and your group will explore the building blocks of the Christian faith through key stories, people, ideas, and teachings in every book of the Bible. You will also explore the bridges and points of connection between the Old and New Testaments.

Choosing and Using the Bible

The central goal of IMMERSION is engaging the members of your group with the Bible in a way that informs their minds, forms their hearts, and transforms the way they live out their Christian faith. Participants will need this study book and a Bible. IMMERSION is an excellent accompaniment to the Common English Bible (CEB). It shares with the CEB four common aims: clarity of language, faith in the Bible's power to transform lives, the emotional expectation that people will find the love of God, and the rational expectation that people will find the knowledge of God.

Other recommended study Bibles include *The New Interpreter's Study Bible* (NRSV), *The New Oxford Annotated Study Bible* (NRSV), *The HarperCollins Study Bible* (NRSV), the *NIV and TNIV Study Bibles*, and the *Archaeological Study Bible* (NIV). Encourage participants to use more than one translation. *The Message: The Bible in Contemporary Language* is a modern paraphrase of the Bible, based on the original languages. Eugene H. Peterson has created a masterful presentation of the Scripture text, which is best used alongside rather than in place of the CEB or another primary English translation.

One of the most reliable interpreters of the Bible's meaning is the Bible itself. Invite participants first of all to allow Scripture to have its say. Pay attention to context. Ask questions of the text. Read every passage with curiosity, always seeking to answer the basic Who? What? Where? When? and Why? questions.

Bible study groups should also have handy essential reference resources in case someone wants more information or needs clarification on specific words, terms, concepts, places, or people mentioned in the Bible. A Bible dictionary, Bible atlas, concordance, and one-volume Bible commentary together make for a good, basic reference library.

The Leader's Role

An effective leader prepares ahead. This leader guide provides easy to follow, step-by-step suggestions for leading a group. The key task of the leader is to guide discussion and activities that will engage heart and head and will invite faith development. Discussion questions are included, and you may want to add questions posed by you or your group. Here are suggestions for helping your group engage Scripture:

State questions clearly and simply.

Ask questions that move Bible truths from "outside" (dealing with concepts, ideas, or information about a passage) to "inside" (relating to the experiences, hopes, and dreams of the participants).

Work for variety in your questions, including compare and contrast, information recall, motivation, connections, speculation, and evaluation.

Avoid questions that call for yes-or-no responses or answers that are obvious.

Don't be afraid of silence during a discussion. It often yields especially thoughtful comments.

Test questions before using them by attempting to answer them yourself.

When leading a discussion, pay attention to the mood of your group by "listening" with your eyes as well as your ears.

Guidelines for the Group

IMMERSION is designed to promote full engagement with the Bible for the purpose of growing faith and building up Christian community. While much can be gained from individual reading, a group Bible study offers an ideal setting in which to achieve these aims. Encourage participants to bring their Bibles and read from Scripture during the session. Invite participants to consider the following guidelines as they participate in the group:

Respect differences of interpretation and understanding.

Support one another with Christian kindness, compassion, and courtesy.

Listen to others with the goal of understanding rather than agreeing or disagreeing.

Celebrate the opportunity to grow in faith through Bible study.

Approach the Bible as a dialogue partner, open to the possibility of being challenged or changed by God's Word.

Recognize that each person brings unique and valuable life experiences to the group and is an important part of the community.

Reflect theologically—that is, be attentive to three basic questions: What does this say about God? What does this say about me/us? What does this say about the relationship between God and me/us?

Commit to a *lived faith response* in light of insights you gain from the Bible. In other words, what changes in attitudes (how you believe) or actions (how you behave) are called for by God's Word?

Group Sessions

The group sessions, like the chapters themselves, are built around three sections: "Claim Your Story," "Enter the Bible Story," and "Live the Story." Sessions are designed to move participants from an awareness of their own life story, issues, needs, and experiences into an encounter and dialogue with the story of Scripture and to make decisions integrating their personal stories and the Bible's story.

The session plans in the following pages will provide questions and activities to help your group focus on the particular content of each chapter. In addition to questions and activities, the plans will include chapter title, Scripture, and faith focus.

Here are things to keep in mind for all the sessions:

Prepare Ahead
Study the Scripture, comparing different translations and perhaps a paraphrase.
Read the chapter, and consider what it says about your life and the Scripture.
Gather materials such as large sheets of paper or a markerboard with markers.
Prepare the learning area. Write the faith focus for all to see.

Welcome Participants
Invite participants to greet one another.
Tell them to find one or two people and talk about the faith focus.
Ask: What words stand out for you? Why?

Guide the Session
Look together at "Claim Your Story." Ask participants to give their reactions to the stories and examples given in each chapter. Use questions from the session plan to elicit comments based on personal experiences and insights.

Ask participants to open their Bibles and "Enter the Bible Story." For each portion of Scripture, use questions from the session plan to help participants gain insight into the text and relate it to issues in their own lives.

Step through the activity or questions posed in "Live the Story." Encourage participants to embrace what they have learned and to apply it in their daily lives.

Invite participants to offer their responses or insights about the boxed material in "Across the Testaments," "About the Scripture," and "About the Christian Faith."

Close the Session

Encourage participants to read the following week's Scripture and chapter before the next session.

Offer a closing prayer.

1. God Credits Us As Righteous—in Spite of Ourselves
Romans 1–4

Faith Focus

The power of God's faithfulness and righteousness overcomes sin's power to divide us from each other and separate us from God.

Before the Session

Paul's letter to the Romans is an important letter because in it Paul presents the totality of his understanding of the way God works with us through Christ Jesus. At the same time, Paul's letter to the Romans is a difficult letter to comprehend, in part because Paul seldom used ten simple words when he could write the same idea in fifty complicated words!

Therefore, don't even think about beginning to lead your study group until you have read and reread Romans in several Bible translations (preferably including a study Bible version such as *The New Interpreter's Study Bible: New Revised Standard Version*). Be sure to read the introductions to the letter in each of those translations. Refresh your memory—or study again—about Paul's world, about the way Jews understood Gentiles, about the law of Moses described in the first five books of the Old Testament and all that had been added to it, and about the other religions that were current in Paul's time. A good resource to use for that is the *Dictionary of Paul and His Letters*, published by InterVarsity Press.

After you've read through Romans in several translations, consider outlining the whole book of Romans, making up *your own* headings and subheadings. Then compare your outline with the outlines presented in a couple of commentaries on Romans.

Claim Your Story

Engage your group in one of two possible ways.

Option One: Ask group members to form groups of three or four to discuss their first reactions on reading Paul's letter to Rome. What were some verses that jumped out as familiar verses? What were some passages that were difficult to comprehend? What seemed to be the overall theme of Paul's argument in Romans?

Option Two: Invite groups of three or four to describe times they felt unworthy. The point is not to share confessions of profound sin, but rather to identify occasions in life when things seemed to suggest that nothing was going to get any better. What was it that pulled them through these dark times and back into the light?

Enter the Bible Story

These initial chapters of Paul's letter to Rome outline Paul's basic understanding of God's will for humanity and the grace that God expressed through Jesus Christ.

The Heart of the Gospel

As a whole group, review this section on pages 10–12. Talk about the three main points the writer makes. Then discuss these questions: Why is the gospel "good" news? Why is the gospel good news for all persons everywhere, not just for some? How can the gospel be good news even for those who do not claim the absolute supremacy of God?

What Went Wrong

In this section, the study writer indicates that God "turned humanity over to its sinning." Probe the meaning of this; then ask group members to discuss the study writer's statement that "God is forbearing." (See page 12.)

In pairs, discuss examples of ways in which we do not honor God and do not thank God, the study writer's summary of Paul's explanation of "what went wrong." Then reflect as a whole group on the often-heard argument that we must follow God's laws in order to experience the peace that passes understanding.

The Law Is Not Enough

What is the study writer's contention regarding why the law was not enough for the Israelites? Now move to our day. Why is the law not enough today? We all know the Golden Rule and the Ten Commandments. Why can we not experience life abundant through these laws, especially if God gave us these laws?

The study writer describes three kinds of persons—Jew, Gentile, and the Gentile who follows the law. What does Paul say about each of these? And how are these three mirrored in our day? In other words, who are the "law-following Jews" of our day? Who are the ignorant-of-the-law Gentiles and the law-following Gentiles of today?

The Gift of Salvation in Christ Is Sufficient/Abraham: The Father of All Who Believe

In groups of four, discuss these questions: If the law is not adequate for our salvation, what is? What did Abraham do that justified him before God and what must we do to be justified before God? Come back to the statement "The gift of salvation in Christ is sufficient." If salvation is a gift, how do our actions affect the giving and the receiving of that gift?

Invite the small groups to share their responses with the total group. Help group members recognize that we live a Christian life and follow God's laws not in fear of what God will do if we don't, but in grateful response to what God has already done in and for us through Christ.

Live the Story

These first four chapters of Paul's letter to the Christians in Rome tell the story of humanity's unworthiness and God's grace. But Paul makes clear that God shows no partiality in offering God's grace to a sinful humanity. This truth reassures each of us that, as the study writer puts it, "our sin is fully accounted for in Christ and we are considered righteous by God. We must hear this refrain loud and clear—All sins are paid for by Christ's work on the cross, and God has declared to each believer the verdict: NOT GUILTY" (page 17). But the flip side of that assurance is that in response, we who are called God's people must offer that good news to *all* as potential brothers and sisters in Christ.

"Consider your church community: where do you see attempts to put up pseudo-markers of spiritual status that act as barriers to the gospel?" (page 17). Talk together about who your congregation welcomes or does not welcome. Then come up with some concrete ways to offer God's grace to *anyone* who comes in contact with your congregation. Pray together for eyes to see and courage to dismantle what might be, for some, obstacles or barriers to receiving the gospel of God's grace.

2. Freed From the Consequences of Sin
Romans 5–6

Faith Focus

Christ's death and resurrection free us from the consequences of sin and make us captive to the way of obedience to God, which leads to right living.

Before the Session

These two chapters in Romans are crucial to Paul's whole discussion of his understanding of justification through faith and the consequences of experiencing that justification. Again, read these chapters in several translations. Consult several commentaries as you prepare to lead discussions of these chapters. Why several commentaries? Because a commentary is a discussion of biblical passages based on one or more person's understandings and interpretations of those passages. Any commentary represents a particular writer or writers' own views about the text. Consequently, reading several commentaries enriches your understanding of biblical texts by providing multiple angles from which to view them.

Claim Your Story

Paul lived in what we might call a "cause and effect" culture. People living in the first century A.D. believed that almost everything that happened was caused by something else and that the effects were automatic and predictable. Thus, Paul and his contemporaries believed that sin (the cause) led to death (the effect) and that this "cause and effect" process was inevitable.

To what extent do you think we see ourselves living in a "cause and effect" culture? What actions would you say inevitably lead to certain effects? In what ways is our concept of "cause and effect" like or unlike the beliefs of Paul and his contemporaries? (One response might be that we continue to believe in causes and effects; but that the effects, while inevitable, may not be immediate.)

Enter the Bible Story
Speaking of Hope

As the study writer points out, Romans 5 commences with a discussion of hope. Paul's notion of hope, however, is not some "pie in the sky" Christmas wish list. So what is Christian hope? Talk about that as a total group. Then consider this statement by the study writer: "Paul emphasizes the firm conviction that God's ultimate plan for the renewed heaven and earth will be a reality" (page 20). How does that statement inform your discussion of Christian hope?

Adam and Christ

What does Adam symbolize in Paul's discussion of humanity's sin? Help group members recall the points of Paul's argument: "(1) that humans can trace their lineage to the first man, Adam, who sinned, (2) that every person is gripped with sin, and (3) that every person faces the consequences of his or her sins, namely death" (page 21). Talk about the implications of seeing ourselves, in terms of our sinful nature, like Adam. Where do you see the truth of the idea that "in Adam" we are all trapped in the power of sin?

Consider this statement by the study writer: "As a consequence of Adam's sin, each person is unable to resist the draw of sin, and thus faces the punishment of death" (page 22). In groups of three, discuss what Paul means by identifying the consequence of our sin as death—does he mean only physical death (which is part of God's plan for all living things) or does Paul mean something more than that? If so, what?

The Way to New Life

If death is the consequence of sin and if we cannot resolve our tendency to sinfulness by our own actions, what is the solution? As the study writer points out so clearly, Paul claims that only by the grace of God manifested in the death and resurrection of Jesus the Christ is our death—physical and spiritual—overcome. Discuss: How would you say your life is changed by recognizing this absolute grace of God? In what ways do you still try to earn or merit God's grace?

Grace and Sin

Paul's discussion of the Mosaic law versus salvation through Jesus Christ sets up a debate that can be joined by the group members. Have the participants form two teams that will debate the value and efficacy of God's "old way" and God's "new way." Printing the arguments on two sides of a large sheet of paper might help the teams keep score and rate the debate.

Grace and Law and the Life of Faith

The assurance of God's grace, according to the study writer, "does not mean that no standards of behavior exist or that righteousness now has no place in our lives as believers. Indeed, Paul argues, grace allows for the achievement of righteous obedience" (page 25). In fact, the study writer continues, "Paul speaks of believers as slaves of righteousness, beholden to its bidding. Paul desires believers to 'be who they are,' to live out the promise of new life" (page 25). Invite group members to share what "righteous obedience" means for them. In living the life of faith in Christ, how do you keep from getting sidetracked into legalism (trying to follow rules) on the one side, and moralism (trying to be good) on the other?

Live the Story

Paul's message is clear and precise: We are justified, made right with God, not through our actions but by the free gift of God's grace in Jesus Christ. That gift frees us from the many kinds of "death" that the group members discussed in the session and enables us to live a new kind of "life" as a willing and eager "slave" of Christ. On the "head" level, this makes sense. But how do we live this out? Discuss as a whole group: How can we live in our twenty-first-century world as servants of God, justified by God's grace, unafraid of any kind of death, embracing the new life in Christ? In other words, how do our words and actions reflect our enslavement to Christ? Or, how do our words and actions reflect our enslavement to something else?

Close by asking persons to pray in silence as they reflect on any changes they might need to make in their lives in order to live fully as slaves of Christ in response to God's gift of grace. Then lead the group in praying the Lord's Prayer.

3. At Once Condemned and Acquitted
Romans 7–8

Faith Focus

The law of sin condemns us, but the Spirit of Christ revokes all charges.

Before the Session

These two chapters of Romans contain at least three ideas that should stimulate discussion. One idea concerns what Paul says about the law, both the problem and the purpose of the law, and how we can understand what Paul says in the context of our day. A second idea emerges from Paul's claim that he does not do the good he wants to do but finds himself doing those things he does not want to do. And a third idea is rooted in Paul's point in Romans 8:28 that "God works all things together for good for the ones who love God." Give careful and prayerful thought to these three concerns and learn all you can about them through commentaries. You are not expected to have all the answers, but you should be able to develop essential questions that will help your group members think beyond surface understandings.

Claim Your Story

Begin this session by raising this question: What were some of the taboos or no-nos you learned as a young child that centered around your family's faith? "Prime the pump" with some of your own recollections, perhaps, "Don't run in the church building," "No going to the movies on Sunday," "Never make a mark in your Bible."

Then move to a discussion of how Paul struggled with the law. Have someone read aloud Romans 7:1-12. Have group members describe in their own words the nature of Paul's struggle with the "rights and wrongs" of the law. Then ask group members to say how rights and wrongs (law) function in their life. How do rights and wrongs affect our understanding of God's love?

As Paul teaches in Chapter 7, while rights and wrongs (law) guide us, they should never be seen as ends in themselves. Why? Because no one can remember, much less keep, all the rights and wrongs, so no one can bring about her or his own salvation by following these rights and wrongs. Why do you think that continues to be a difficult concept for us to get?

Enter the Bible Story
The Tension Between the Law and the Spirit

The study writer explores the tension between the law and the Spirit by highlighting how Paul contrasts the law written on stone and the law within our hearts. But, claims the study writer, "We cannot *keep* the law fully ... for sin is more powerful than our wills" (page 30). Explore this statement. If sin is more powerful than our wills, then why should we try to resist sin? What is the answer to our inability to resist sin? And how does the written law contrast with the law within our hearts in terms of helping us resist sin? Be careful! Note that the study writer reminds us that right intentions do not absolve us of our responsibility for our sinfulness: the old adage, "it's the thought that counts" won't cut it. Why not?

No Condemnation for Those Who Are in Christ Jesus

Ask a group member to read Romans 8:1-3 aloud. What does Paul's joyous announcement mean? Does it mean we no longer sin? Does it mean that sin no longer tempts us? Does it mean that sin does not exist any longer? If we have been rescued from sin, then why do we have to follow the law (the law of Moses) or any law?

Suffering in the Present Age

After Paul's great opening in Chapter 8, he acknowledges the reality of suffering and pain in the world, and by inference, in the lives of the faithful. Why does Paul address the issue of suffering from the perspective of creation? How does his argument that "our present sufferings rank as insignificant when compared to our future glory" (page 34) speak to our own attempts to avoid suffering at all costs?

Sharing in Christ's Likeness

Finally, Paul proclaims with great confidence that "God works all things together for good for the ones who love God." Consider this verse (8:28) in the light of Romans 8:38-39. If in fact 8:28 does not mean that everything that happens to us is good, positive, and constructive, then what exactly does it mean? How has that single verse informed (or how can it inform) your faith?

Live the Story

One of Paul's most magnificent statements is his summary of his discussion of the law and of life in the Spirit despite trials and tribulations, despite personal failures and the inability to always do the right thing. This summary is Romans 8:38-39: "I'm convinced that nothing can separate us from God's love in Christ Jesus our Lord: not death or life, not angels or rulers, not present things or future things, not powers or height or depth, or any other thing that is created." Ask several good readers to read these two verses aloud from as many translations as are available in your group. Pause after each reading to let the words soak in. Then invite group members to memorize these two verses by reciting them aloud several times in unison. Commit as a group to living in the Spirit by and through this glorious promise.

4. God Chooses All Who Call on God's Name
Romans 9–11

Faith Focus
God alone faithfully and mercifully chooses all those who call on God's name to receive salvation.

Before the Session
These chapters of Paul's letter to Rome may appear, on a cursory reading, to be convoluted arguments that have little reference to us today. But take your time, read these three chapters slowly and carefully, refer to several commentaries, and then reflect on these chapters in this way: imagine that Paul is not talking about Jews and Gentiles, but instead about who is "in" and who is "out." Imagine, for instance, that the "Jews" about whom Paul speaks, are present-day Christians. Imagine that the "Gentiles" in Paul's mind are in fact adherents of other religions, say Muslims, Sikhs, or Hindus. As you study and discuss these chapters, pay attention to Paul's emphasis on God's unlimited grace for all of God's children, regardless of the religious differences between them.

Claim Your Story
A preacher once said, "When I get to heaven, I'm going to be surprised by all the folks who are there that I never thought would make it!"

You might begin your session with this lighthearted comment as an introduction to a discussion of Romans 9–11. For the crux of these chapters is what determines who is in and who is out.

Form groups of three or four and invite them to consider this question: If Paul were writing to us today and speaking, as he does in these three chapters, of Jews and Gentiles, about whom might he be referring? Come together as a total group to share responses to that question. Then together brainstorm what other groups of persons today reflect the differences that separated Jews and Gentiles in Paul's day.

Enter the Bible Story
God's Faithfulness to Israel
The study writer observes, "Throughout Romans 9–11, a scarlet thread of God's mercy has been woven" (page 44). Indeed, these chapters proclaim God's mercy in many ways. But Paul approaches this theme from several different angles.

First, Paul describes God's faithfulness to Israel, faithfulness to a people who in so many ways had failed to keep their part of the covenant. Pose this question for discussion by the whole group: To what extent have we who have lived as Christians all our lives failed to keep covenant with God, just as the Israelites did? Then ask, as Paul did: "What's the advantage of being a Christian?" Allow time for the group to explore their responses. Help group members understand that our heritage as Christians equips us to know and respond to God's love for us through Christ; but our heritage as Christians alone does not justify us before God any more than attempted obedience to the law justified the Jews of Paul's day.

God's Plan of Salvation

Quickly review this section (pages 42–43). Then, in groups of three or four, discuss this question and search for illustrations and examples: In what ways do contemporary Christians—including ourselves—follow their own plan of salvation rather than following God's plan? Note: in order for people to deal with this question, they will need to distinguish God's plan of salvation from humanly- (or denominationally-) imposed requirements for salvation. Hear responses from the groups. Be sure to press for illustrations and examples.

No Distinction Between Jew and Greek/The Scarlet Thread of God's Mercy

According to the study writer, Paul warns his Gentile readers against "triumphalism" (page 44). Take time to be sure everyone is clear on the meaning of that term. Then discuss these questions: Where do you see evidence of triumphalism in our day? What forms of expression does it take? To whom might Christians feel superior? How can we as Christians guard against triumphalism in our dealing with others?

Conclude this portion of the discussion by recalling that Chapters 9 through 11 of Paul's letter to the Romans focus on Paul's own people, the Jews. But these chapters are a metaphor for all of us. All of us can trace our lineage back to God, and all of us have violated God's commandments again and again. But Paul describes even more emphatically God's righteousness and God's infinite mercy. God's mercy and forgiveness is the prevailing theme of the Old and New Testaments. God's willingness to forgive us is the underlying theme of the Scriptures. Thus, the story of God's forgiveness and infinite love are highlighted through these chapters and through our lives as we experience that complete forgiveness and reconciliation. Ask those who feel comfortable sharing to describe the ways they have experienced in their own lives the "scarlet thread of God's mercy."

Live the Story

In many ways, Paul lived in a world much like ours: a world where groups of people distrusted one another, saw one another as enemies or threats, or felt themselves superior to one another. Help the group recognize that the basic thrust of these key chapters in Romans is that God's salvation does not require membership in a particular group, but depends wholly on God's grace. Ask group members to be aware during this coming week of all the strangers they encounter and to recognize that each of these strangers, regardless of the conditions under which they might be living, is a child of God, redeemed and saved by God's grace—and therefore a sister or brother in Christ.

5. A Community Shaped by Sacrificial Love
Romans 12–13

Faith Focus

In faithful and obedient response to God's grace, we live as a community shaped by sacrificial love.

Before the Session

Go ahead and take a deep breath. You and your group have wrestled with the toughest and densest of Paul's arguments. In these two chapters of Romans, Paul is more direct and straightforward.

In a way, Paul could have opened these chapters with the word "Therefore." In the first eleven chapters, he presented his theology, his understanding of the ways in which God has redeemed all of humanity by God's grace through Jesus Christ; and now in these chapters Paul is saying, in effect, "Once you've comprehended the way God works with us through Christ Jesus, this is how we ought to live in response to God's grace and love." Make no mistake, however, these chapters of practical instruction are every bit as important as Paul's exposition of theology in the first eleven chapters. Paul's counsel about right living deserves our close attention.

Claim Your Story

Where and how did you learn how to live in harmony with others? Invite your group members to respond to that question. Encourage them to think of rules of everyday conduct that they learned early in life. Where did they learn them? From parents? teachers? in Sunday School? or perhaps in other places? Some might refer to such things as the Boy Scout or Girl Scout Motto or the Golden Rule or the Ten Commandments.

Then follow up that discussion by posing this question: If we all learned similar principles of living in harmony with others, what keeps us from consistently living by them?

Enter the Bible Story

Begin this session by reading aloud the following excerpt from page 49:

"Beginning in Romans 12, Paul points back to the mercies of God that he explained in Chapter 11, those extended to everyone, because everyone has been disobedient. This mercy, Paul urges, requires our response of faith and submission. Paul calls it 'living sacrifice,' which is an oxymoron, as every sacrifice is by definition dead."

In groups of three or four, discuss these questions: What does the word *sacrifice* mean in today's world? If a sacrifice is something we do with some reluctance, then in what ways are we "living sacrifices"? How do our faith and our submission to God define our lives as "living sacrifices"?

A Living Sacrifice

The study writer lists five ways we can understand and do God's will. Have the group name these five ways: (1) the guidance of the Holy Spirit, (2) the interceding of Christ on our behalf, (3) access to God through prayer, (4) the Bible, and (5) the church. Ask for illustrations or examples of each one. Pay particular attention to the fourth and fifth ways (the Bible and the church); encourage group members to describe ways in which they have come to understand and do God's will through the guidance of the Bible and through the help of Christian sisters and brothers. How has the church taught, admonished, and encouraged you?

The Body of Christ

The study writer indicates that Christians have been "tempted to see their spiritual development in individualistic terms" (page 51). Talk together about why this is so. Ask: Would you say your church emphasizes individual salvation or community salvation? Explain your answers. What does it mean to say, "Paul emphasizes that transformation occurs in community" (page 51)? What kind of transformation is Paul talking about? What kind of community does he mean? Again, encourage the group to provide examples and illustrations of their answers.

The Body of Christ, Gifted for Action

If indeed we are "gifted for action," how can we learn to value the gifts each person brings to community without valuing some more highly than others? Read aloud Romans 12:9-13, recalling that Paul's point is that love must be sincere. Talk about what this kind of love looks like (or should look like) in our lives.

The Body of Christ and the Body Politic

To what extent are Paul's comments about believers yielding to government authority appropriate for us today? Recall these words from page 54: "We 'help' other drivers not get caught speeding by flashing our lights to warn them of police officers ahead of them. We lie about our children's ages to get them into a movie more cheaply. Paul knows that this sort of behavior is a recipe for disaster, both on a personal and a social level."

Where have you seen evidence of such "disasters"? Why do we work so hard to avoid submitting to authorities?

Live the Story

Read aloud Romans 13:11-14. Then tell this story: The famous evangelist Billy Graham was once asked when he thought Christ was coming again. Graham answered that he was living today in expectation that Christ is coming today. But what if Christ does not come today was the next question posed by the inquirer. Graham answered, "Then I'll live tomorrow in expectation that Christ is coming tomorrow!"

Ask each group member to pray in silence for guidance and direction from the Holy Spirit to determine what transformation she or he might need to make to "put on the Lord Jesus Christ" and to be fully ready if Christ comes today.

Invite the group members to pray aloud "A Covenant Prayer in the Wesleyan Tradition":

I am no longer my own, but thine.
Put me to what thou wilt, rank me with whom thou wilt.
Put me to doing, put me to suffering.
Let me be employed by thee or laid aside for thee,
exalted for thee or brought low by thee.
Let me be full, let me be empty.
Let me have all things, let me have nothing.
I freely and heartily yield all things
to thy pleasure and disposal.
And now, O glorious and blessed God,
Father, Son, and Holy Spirit,
thou art mine, and I am thine. So be it.
And the covenant which I have made on earth,
let it be ratified in heaven. Amen.[1]

1. From *The United Methodist Hymnal,* 607 (The United Methodist Publishing House, 1989).

6. God's Welcome, Our Response
Romans 14–16

Faith Focus

By extending God's welcome to each other, we bring unity and peace to God's people.

Before the Session

This session completes your group's study of Paul's epistle to the Romans. Romans is at once a crucial book of the New Testament and a challenging text for Bible students. Thinkers and theologians from Augustine to Barth have wrestled with it and felt they had not fully grasped its import and insight. Therefore, do not let this end your consideration of Romans. Resolve to return to it and reread it often; pray with it and over it; let the richness of its content and language inform your growing faith and discipleship. Encourage your group members to do the same. May the words and ideas of Romans live in you and in the members of your study group.

Claim Your Story

Paul says some difficult things in the three chapters considered in this session. For example, Paul reminds us that we have no right to judge others or to pass judgment on the ways others might be living. Can this be true in every case? Ask group members to cite examples and illustrations of times and situations in which we may be called upon to judge the conduct of others. Do we not judge and correct the actions of our children? Do not school teachers judge the efforts of their students? Do we not sometimes judge the apparently outrageous (to us!) behavior of teenagers? So what is Paul really saying here? What exactly is he encouraging and discouraging?

Enter the Bible Story
The Christian Life: Walking in Love

Recall the material in this section on pages 60–61. Call the group's attention to how the writer describes Paul's concerns regarding observing special days and eating certain kinds of meat. As a whole group, discuss how Paul's suggestions might apply to the present day. What are some of the issues that separate us that the study writer might describe as "neutral in terms of faith"? For example, to what extent is the way we celebrate the Lord's Supper or practice the sacrament of baptism "neutral in terms of faith"? Or are issues like this central to our faith?

The study writer suggests that "Paul is not talking about looking the other way when sinful behaviors are going on" (page 61). When and how do we "look the other way when sinful behaviors are going on"? How do we determine which behaviors are sinful and which behaviors are "neutral in terms of faith"? When members of the same community of faith disagree agree on which behaviors are which, how should they resolve (or live with) the differences?

The Christian Life: Accountable to God

Read aloud and then discuss this statement: "Our disobedience will not result in lost salvation, but it will be judged at the Last Judgment" (page 62). If our salvation will not be lost, what will be lost? What is your view of the Last Judgment? Will it be an individual or a corporate judgment? That is, will we be judged individually or as a church or both? How does the study writer suggest Christians prepare for the Last Judgment? What form would you say your own preparation for the Last Judgment takes?

Recall this observation from page 62: "Just as we trip and stumble if we are not paying attention to where we are going, so too if we lose our focus on our Savior, we easily fall into criticism and judgmental attitudes." Then share responses to this question: What distractions tempt you to take your eyes off the Lord? What personal preferences might have you elevated to the status of "gospel truth"?

The Christian Life: Patience and Peace Over Power and Politics

Christ welcomes us into the family of his followers, and we must do likewise for others. Talk together about who is included in the "others" we are to welcome. Who in our community might find being welcomed into our church family difficult or painful? Who in our community might not be welcomed at all? How do you think we as Christians are called to respond to this?

Plans and Instructions

Invite group members to share stories about their realization that plans changed or gone awry are evidence of God's planning for their lives. Ask how they came to recognize God's greater wisdom and how they accepted a plan different from their own.

Live the Story

Take time to recall the six-week study of Romans and the various verses that come to mind or the key themes that caught your attention. Invite your group to consider how much of Paul's letter has shaped their thinking as Christians. What of Paul's many admonitions throughout his letter do you need to heed? Talk about how you will follow his advice.

The study writer says, "In the Letter to the Romans, Paul shows God's offer of freedom in Christ, freedom from drawing our self-worth from comparisons with others, freedom to love and serve without thinking of what we will gain in return, freedom with fellow believers to appreciate how vast is God's love and care for his children" (page 67). Allow the group a few moments of silence to think about how they will use this freedom in Christ to serve others—in their family; in their congregation; in their community. Provide blank bookmarks for each person to use to write down his or her decisions. Encourage them to keep the bookmarks in their Bibles in a section of the Book of Romans.